A PROFESSOR TAKES TO THE SEA

LEARNING THE ROPES ON THE NATIONAL GEOGRAPHIC EXPLORER
VOLUME I "EPIC SOUTH AMERICA" 2013

MARK J. CURRAN

Trafford rev. 05/08/2018

 www.trafford.com

North America & international
toll-free: 1 888 232 4444 (USA & Canada)
fax: 812 355 4082

TABLE OF CONTENTS

PREFACE

FROM THE CLASSROOM TO THE "CIRCLE OF TRUTH" – THE SPEAKER'S PODIUM ON THE "NATIONAL GEOGRAPHIC EXPLORER"

Lindblad-National Geographic Expeditions is the renowned name for quality trips to see the best of nature in the world. Its seven-ship fleet, <u>circa</u> 2013, with amazing crew and support staff, travels the seven seas with outstanding expedition leaders, naturalists, National Geographic photographers and guest expedition speakers, all on board to provide the guests with an outstanding experience. In past years and more so today, the company has provided the guests with a cultural experience as well – expertise on the history and culture of the places visited – this in addition to the expected science, nature and photography presented by the staff. The vehicle is the round speaker's podium in the lounge of the Explorer, called by the staff "The Circle of Truth."

I'm a retired Arizona State University Professor of Languages and Literature. Although my field of expertise is Spanish Language and Brazilian Portuguese Language and their respective cultures, specialization was Brazil – its literature, history, religion, politics and folklore, the latter best seen in its folk-popular poetry, "a literatura de cordel" and its relation to erudite literature and history. Brazil will be the connection to LEX (Lindblad Expeditions) and the Explorer.

There will be three stories: Volume I will be the "Epic South America" trip with my participation from Brazil to Uruguay and Buenos Aires; Volume II will be the first Atlantic Crossing plus the shorter trip to Brazil, Uruguay and Buenos Aires in 2014 and the "Atlantic 108" Crossing of 2016. In Volume II any repeated stops will be summarized, but new experiences and important moments will all be documented. Enjoy.

It is important to add this note to Volume I: while life aboard the Explorer will be the focus of part of the narrative, my own research on the places we visited in 2013, 2014 and 2016 and the account of the excursions in Brazil, Uruguay and Argentina will be a large part of this book, as well as the images in the book.

As mentioned, this book in two volumes which I hope to be both informative and entertaining needs a bit of explanation as to content and format. As part-time staff on three expeditions of Lindblad – National Geographic on the National Geographic Explorer I write as former employee, eager participant and chronicler of voyages. There are stipulations I must follow due to reasons of privacy and copyright by my employer, guidelines I follow rigorously.

There will be no mention of names of guests and no specific photos of them, except in the case of appearance as distant background to my own photos of the trips. I do hope to occasionally include vignettes of conversation with some guests which enrich the narrative but do not infringe on privacy. After all, it was a major aspect of my job to spend time with them aboard ship and on shore excursions and to engage them in helpful conversation especially at meals. Due to my age as a retiree we almost always got along well and had much in common to share.

The names of crew members on the Explorer, of Expedition Leaders, Staff and Naturalists will appear, as well as titles of their amazing presentations, but no detailed content or quotation of the presentations or accompanying photos or images will appear. Photos of said persons will appear as they were integral to the trips. I have written permissions from all concerned.

Equally important and with similar treatment are the guest speakers, famous people, all international experts, who enriched the Expedition Experience and my conversations with them. Being a university professor with long years of teaching and lecturing, of writing both scholarly and travel articles and books, I was truly humbled in their presence, as it were, a "small fish in a very big pond." Figuratively and literally.

My own presentations and notes will appear since the copyright on them is of course owned by me. I believe they contributed to the trips and my own role as staff. Informative vignettes on images from places visited are an important part of this book. In one instance extensive travel notes on Portugal will be added to the narrative as an addendum to the 2016 Atlantic Crossing and travel in Madeira.

What I can tell in all candor are the trials, the tribulations and later small successes of learning the ropes as staff on the Explorer. There were many surprises, some difficult moments created by the job but also due to my inexperience that may add some "color" to the narrative. Veterans of LEX trips may get a laugh out of the latter.

Finally, I want to add that the narration itself, although generally chronological, is basically what came up, what happened, most of it new to me. The Table of Contents is thus not that of chapters of a book but of a detailed list of events as they happened, people I met and what we saw. Interspersed in the narration when Explorer departs from Belém do Pará in Brazil and arrives in Buenos Aires are many days AT SEA with their own routine, surprises and adventures. AT SEA really provided the education for all.

LINDBLAD EXPEDITIONS – NATIONAL GEOGRAPHIC "EPIC JOURNEY TO SOUTH AMERICA"

October 2013

The National Geographic Explorer Ship

INTRODUCTION

This wonderful retirement "gig" in 2013 began a few months earlier with a simple phone call. The person calling was Jen Martin, in charge of recruitment for on-board staff for the LINDBLAD EXPEDITIONS - NATIONAL GEOGRAPHIC trips. She basically explained the company to me (I knew little about it at the time): the fleet of seven expedition (not "cruise") ships, the partnership with National Geographic Society and details I do not recall at this writing. She said she knew of me by my Trafford Book "Adventures of a 'Gringo' Researcher in Brazil in the 1960s."

Jen had read the book and thought I would be a suitable candidate to come aboard to provide cultural presentations about Brazil on this major trip for 2013 marking the 125th Anniversary of the National Geographic Society – an "Epic"' Trip along the east shore of South America. I would come on board at Belém do Pará, Brazil, near the mouth of the Amazon and remain on board until Buenos Aires at the end of the trip. Jen outlined a few of the duties, but it was all pretty sketchy for me the newcomer at that time. After a 45 - minute phone call which turned out to be an interview she said, "We might as well formalize this conversation and have you confirmed for the trip." I recall that I emphasized that I could provide entertaining, informative talks with great enthusiasm and thanked her.

The rest as they say is "history." As a naïve, totally "green" staff member I would join the National Geographic Explorer ship with a truly amazing ship crew and Lindblad staff of naturalists, cultural experts, undersea divers, and first rate and famous photographers on what turned out to be just the first of three such trips. Sometimes you live right.

What followed in the ensuing months was a lot of intense work on the presentations (I offered a list, Jen approved, and I began the work); these were cultural presentations on many aspects of Brazil, most based on what I had been teaching or writing about for years. The main task was to find, reproduce and prepare the images for the talks, most of them luckily scanned from slides years earlier when I was planning writing projects. I was by choice not yet a user of Power Point, so the photos were simply set up in folders according to topic, put on DVDs or flash drives and were just the beginning of an "audio-visual" Odyssey the next four years. This first trip turned out to be special for indeed I had an important role to play, plenty of opportunity to share expertise and very positive results from both staff and guests.

At the same time at home in Colorado all the nuts and bolts for the trip took place, and I note that LEX from the very beginning walked me through the steps for passport renewal, special 10 - year Business Visa to Brazil, Seaman's Card, tetanus and diphtheria shots and yellow fever renewal shot. There was more: the actual travel arrangements, but the LEX staff took me through it all without a hitch; theirs was an amazing team of specialists, but of course keep in mind this was a business many years old and probably number one in the world in "Expedition Trips." It was sometime after the call that I received a copy of the Staff Manual with all the details: line of command on the trips, duties of each type of staff member, comportment, salary and "extras" and tight regulations regarding professional behavior and the copyright situation limiting what could be shared about the trip, the passengers ("guests") and the like. The latter would become important to me later when considering a book for Trafford on the experiences. So it went and I was ready to go!

The time I was first "on duty" was September 30 to October 24, 2013. The "rookie" analogy to baseball is not misplaced as one sees in the following pages.

TRAVEL TO BRAZIL

September 30, 2013

I received a call at our house in Mesa, Arizona, from Desirae in the LEX travel office and she said, "There is a change in ship schedule due to the turn out to Paramaribo, Suriname (formerly Dutch Guiana) to get a passenger and spouse off the ship, he having suffered a serious illness and the only available hospital being at Paramaribo where he would be transferred by Swiss Air to home for surgery." I later learned some good advice for guests: get travel insurance or an evacuation may cost thousands of dollars. I would therefore leave one day early. It turned out later that the ship could make up the one-day delay, so I would not have had to leave when I did, but the good news is I got a free day in Belém do Pará capital of the State of Pará, Brazil, for tourism.

Everything on this venture was a surprise for the newcomer. Among the first is that staff are often called upon to take things to the ship: passports, documents, prescription medicines and the like. My bags were already jammed with little extra space and Desirae called again, this time for me to take rather large video camera batteries for the ship videographer. The inconvenient request (on my part) turned out okay because Lindblad concluded the videographer could get the equipment sent down via a LEX staff member flying from Miami, Florida and meeting us in Rio de Janeiro. However, they still needed the prescription medicines a "guest" had forgotten in the U.S. The UPS medicines arrived five minutes before I left on Super Shuttle to the airport in Phoenix. I left a note with the gracious neighbor Mary Jane Przybyla who dealt with Lindblad on yet another package that she would have to send back to LEX for me. The persons who needed the medicine would thank me on board.

Super Shuttle almost did not get me to the Phoenix airport on time: the van blew a tire on a freeway and we all nervously waited for another van to pick us up, a harrowing beginning of the trip. I recall the deafening traffic noise as we all stood aside four lanes of rushing traffic west of the bridge in Tempe. The van came, we still arrived with some time to spare, the Delta line was short, and a kind, understanding clerk overrode the $75 baggage charge to São Paulo (LEX had routed me to São Paulo, a destination on the international flights, and from there I would fly five hours back north to Belém to board the ship.)

I bought one of those "crummy" lunches on board Delta to Atlanta and spent the time reading the Lindblad Staff Manual (like my young wife Keah would read the Portuguese 101 textbook on her way to Brazil in 1970). I took the terminal train in Atlanta to the International Wing and Delta, noting the usual sloppiness of the way travelers dress these days – it's dismal.

The international flight was just "okay" with a TV style supper and two Heinekens, lots of talk with a young Mormon Missionary, age nineteen, from Parker, Colorado, on his way with colleagues to Belo Horizonte for the mission. I had taught the return missionaries for years in language and culture classes at Arizona State University. How young, naïve and uneducated they were at the start of the missions! No so at the end!

The engine noise of the jets was loud, we were jammed in the "cattle car" seats, so there was zero sleep! The travel was not fun, but I at least spent some time remembering the "good old days" of research travel to Brazil beginning in the 1960s when it was fun. The plane was jammed, and at least they offered a pillow and blanket, but no traveler's kit with tooth brush, slippers, sleep mask, or maps like the olden days. So, we arrived in smoggy São Paulo.

The LEX-NATIONAL GEOGRAPHIC contact person was right there outside the international travelers' gate with his "Curran" sign and had all the proper paper work done. I showed my Sea Man's Card, passport and there was no bag inspection. So, all was loaded on the GOL (the modern, evolved Brazilian Airline from the old Varig Company, headquarters in Minas Gerais State) flight to Belém. An aside: the Brazilian entry permit one is supposed to keep for departure disappeared in the shuffle by the LEX staff in Belém, auspicious or not? Esther the Explorer Purser on board the ship said they would do another one, but we left Brazil by ship and Argentina was the exit, so it became a non - issue.

There was great people watching in the São Paulo airport waiting for the Belém flight; folks here were more dressed up for travel than in the casual, scruffy United States. On the other hand, there was Brazilian chaos – a constant shifting of gates to the last minute (I understand this is normal and a constant complaint of Brazilian air travelers). The airport itself was crowded and run down. I finally got aboard the 737 to Belém. "I am exhausted."

On the GOL flight, we were cramped like sardines. I got a middle seat. The meal service took the entire two and one-half hours – one crew member for the entire plane, and this for a simple sandwich. Oh, the good ole' days – see my description of Varig from Rio to Recife in 1966. The slowdown was because of modern technology – each passenger was forced to use a single credit card machine. It was lousy!

TRAVEL TO AND ARRIVAL IN BELEM - IT ALL TURNED AROUND!
October 1st

Belém do Pará is the capital of the northern Brazilian state of Pará; it was founded in 1616 by the Portuguese with the idea of combatting French, Dutch and English trade excursions in the area. It is located on the Pará River, 100 miles from the mouth of the Amazon, the huge island of Marajó between the two rivers. Originally the main port for the export of rubber from the upstream rubber boom territory of Pará and Amazonas States (and the important port of Manaus), it later became important for the export of the huge iron ore deposits of Carajás in Pará State. Today it is still important for exports but as well for tourism and the most famous religious festival in Brazil – the "Círio" de Nazaré – or festival of the Virgin of Nazaré [Nazareth].

Much of the following text comes from diary notes, so may vary from present to past tense.

My god it has changed and grown since my last visit with wife Keah in 1970. They have invested in and modernized the "cidade velha" or old downtown Belém. The original port was moved 150 kilometers to the east along the coast and is a major shipping area receiving iron ore, etc. from the interior (one imagines Carajás). It was nice for tourism. Belém lost said port some twenty years ago, so they are renovating the old river port area for tourism (it is called "As Docas" or "The Docks") and this includes all the famous churches. I tour tomorrow and will tell if it is indeed better.

I am lodged in the upscale Hilton on the main avenue in downtown Belém. I was complimented on my Portuguese by the GOL pilot checking out as I headed in. I found the next day the old hotel I stayed in in 1966, and again with wife Keah in 1970, now converted to a business on Belém's main street, Avenida Getúlio Vargas in the business area.

The Hilton is centrally located, walking distance to the Teatro da Paz and the central plaza, "A Praça da República," just across the street. There were bleachers lining the street, all in preparation for the upcoming "Círio de Nazaré" festival, the largest of the year in these parts. It is a blowout! A huge affair! It begins October 13th, so I am only two days early; I wrote of it in my 1966 "Adventures" book.

My chauffer from LEX, off-duty and for a fee, will drive me around town tomorrow and be my tour guide ["cicerone"]. The temperature is 90 degrees and humid! Bruno is my man.

The hotel is very modern, a very nice room. An unexpected benefit – at 6 p.m. each day there are snacks and REAL scotch in a lounge (this is actually a small but important cultural note for Brazil: for long-time Brazil travelers the local "ersatz" scotch was a headache in more than one way). Maybe that explains why Brazilians themselves prefer "choppe" draft beer or the national sugar cane rum drink "caipirinha." The "cocktail hour" is included in the daily room rate, a first for me in Brazil. There is also a "free" buffet breakfast in the a.m. It should be at 330 "reais" tariff per day.

The National Geographic Explorer ship is supposed to be in tomorrow October 2nd or the 3rd. No one seems to know its arrival time. I am hoping I have time to do tourism on my own. I shall know tomorrow a.m.

I think Belém has proved to be very smart. There of course is the normal poverty, but it turns out to be a wonderful place to see. Exhausted and to sleep at 8:30 p.m. Let's see what tomorrow brings.

TOURISM ON MY OWN IN BELÉM

October 2nd

I slept from 8:30 p.m. to 8:30 a.m. Shave, demitasse "instant coffee" in the room before heading down to the lobby restaurant for breakfast – orange juice, piña, fruit salad, ham, cheese, French break, "pão de acapiçu" (like cheese bread), great "café com leite, bolo de chocolate."

I called Bruno and he picked me up at 10:00 a.m. We walked at my request on Avenida Presidente Vargas, past our old "Hotel do Central," now surrounded by shops. The street is lined with "mangueiras" – beautiful huge shade trees - and stores. (Note that much of this tourism, but not all was done by the guests of the Explorer when it would dock a day later.)

We walked through the commerce to the port on the "Bahia do Guajará." There were some ships, but the "new" main port is to the north and east. On the big island to the north is the Petrobras Station. There are big oil cargo ships in the "Baia Guarujá" off to the west of downtown. (This is where I saw the Amazon cargo ships ["cargueiros"] and swim race in 1967.) Unlike the Ver-O-Peso ("Check the Weight") market scene in those old days there are no Japanese - Brazilians in sight; I understand they now live in towns far away in the interior. I saw a documentary on the Japanese agriculture in 2014 and it showed all kinds of fruit production, etc. sent to fruit and juice stands throughout Brazil. At least for me, the Japanese no longer were a visible presence in the old market at Belém this time around.

Our ship will dock in the old port mentioned.

Perhaps it is fitting that my first photo of Belém features President Getúlio Vargas, Brazil's most famous president who ruled in the 1930s, first as a democratic elected president, then a dictator modeling his government on Portugal's long-time dictator Antônio de Salazar in the 1940s of WW II time, then his overthrow by the Brazilian military, and finally his return as a "Democratic" president in the 1950s. The era closed unhappily with his suicide in 1954 in the national presidential palace (the Catete Palace) in Rio de Janeiro, a victim of old-time Brazilian crony politics.

The statue of President Getúlio Vargas (with birds and bird droppings on top) was a very undignified fate for Brazil's most famous president. So, the old "port" is gone, but replacing it are the new "Docas" - the tourist center, cafés, and restaurants.

There is a new "reformed" Ver-o-Peso" ["Check the Weight"] Market, not with the old wooden market stands ["barracas"] but stands with plastic roofs. The vultures ["urubús"] are still there; descendants surely of the ones I saw in 1967 and 1970.

In the market we saw vegetables, chiles, home remedies for sex including Viagra natural substitute, "farofa" or manioc flour, huge bins of shrimp, and Pirarucú fish (this is the huge Amazon fish Brazilian iconic playwright Ariano Suassuna tells tall stories about in "The Rogues' Trial" and the one I saw dragged onto the "milk boat" and tossed below into the hold in Manaus in 1967). We went back in to see the fish market, ten kinds at least! The fishing boats come in at 4 a.m.; this is when you get the best price.

Shrimp at the Ver O Peso Market

Natural Viagra at the Belém Market

HISTORIC BELÉM AND DEFENSE OF THE CITY

We walked by the passenger boats, fishing boats, and the fort of 1617 built to defend the Portuguese colony from all manner of foreign incursion from the Spanish, the French, the Dutch and the English scourge of all South America, Sir Francis Drake! Known today as the "Forte do Castelo," its history is truly amazing – attacks on the original wooden fort by Tupinambá Indians in the 17th century, constant attacks by the French, Dutch and English vying for control of Belém's important location on the entrance to the Amazon River throughout colonial days, attack by mercenary British troops in the hire of the Crown of Portugal during Brazil's effort at independence from Portugal, and finally a refuge for the tens of thousands of persons fleeing from the droughts in Brazil's northeast in the twentieth century. There were cannons, a museum of the Ilha do Marajó Indians, herons, and a view of Ver – o – Peso.

Guide Bruno and myself then were off to the church of "Alexandre," the old Jesuit Church, 16th – 17th century; there were no photos allowed but we saw dark wood, beautifully carved altars with images of angels ["anjos"]. It was a bit like the "Igreja de São Francisco" in Bahia, Brazil but without paint, gold gilt.

Nearby was the "Igreja da Sé," the cathedral, with mass, sermon, and girls singing in the pulpits.

We would then walk through the old city ["cidade velha"] and its commerce. Our lunch was an introduction to a recent phenomenon of Brazilian cuisine: "lunch by the kilo" ["almoço pelo kilo]" - "galinha, bife, farofa, arroz, feijão, e suco de laranja," 16 reais for the two of us.

THE BASILICA OF NAZARÉ – HISTORY AND IMPORTANCE

Bruno and I walked back to the Hilton, got in his car and drove to the "Basílica de Nazaré." This was important for me – my cordelian poetry in 1966 told of the festival. The "festa" is for thirty days beginning October 13. It's "farra e religião!" - partying and religion! There is a great street parade and it's "Carnival in Belém." One can read my old description of it from a folk poetry broadside from 1966! In sum, the festival is the largest of its kind in all Brazil and based on legend of course; it marks the importance of the "Virgem do Nazaré" image, the cult and ritual to her, the miracles, the establishment of the Basilica, and finally the festival itself. It's often termed "Brazil's Carnival in the North" and draws national and international tourists and "wannabe" movie and TV stars to see and be seen during the 30-day party.

After the Nazaré experience Bruno dropped me off at the hotel, saying "anytime" (for a fee). There was yet another shower after all the humidity. Not wanting to waste the limited time in Belém, I then took off on another walking jaunt on "Presidente Vargas" Avenue in front of the hotel where I met a "cordel" poet from Paraíba State on the bulge in northeastern Brazil who travels by airplane and sells his wares to newspapers stands ["bancas de jornais"]. The story-poem is placed in a plastic envelope and displayed alongside newspapers and magazines. It appears everyone now, the general public that is, is at least aware of "cordel," a huge change from my early research days. The poet José travels from Paraíba to Fortaleza, São Luis, Belém, Manaus, and Boa Vista in the far West of the Amazon Region. This was unheard of in 1966 when the poets still traveled by mule or horseback or on third class buses to the markets. And it was still a bit of a leap of faith in 2013 to imagine a humble folk-popular poet thusly selling his wares.

Later there were cocktails back at the hotel where I meet Romeu from Belo Horizonte in Minas Gerais State. He represents two firms, one U.S., the other French, that sell blood services (a Brazilian blood bank) in Minas Gerais, all the Northeast and North. He travels from Alagoas to Macapá, Manaus, Boa Vista and Roraima in far western Brazil. He has two daughters, and both attend Catholic school in Minas operated by Spanish nuns. The older girl studies "cordel" in school brought in by the nuns! The changes in Brazil are incredible; "cordel" would have never been allowed in my early research days because of its "folk, low status." The girl studies piano, classical. He allows no I-pod with headphones. We had great rapport, wonderful.

Felt good to be back in the room, steak sandwich and "batata frita."

Wander (that is a Brazilian first name), representative of LEX-NGEO comes at 5 p.m., gathers my passport, Sea Man's Card, entry papers and takes them to customs ["alfândega"] and police to "free me tomorrow" ["liberar-me amanhã"] to get on the ship, supposedly by 8 – 8:30 a.m. All this is like being on another planet. I shower and pack for the ship.

TRANSFER TO THE NATIONAL GEOGRAPHIC EXPLORER AND INTRODUCTION TO THE SHIP October 4th

I was up at 6:30, had the big buffet breakfast, and watched TV news until 8:30. Wander the LEX agent meets me and takes me to the ship. There is a delay at the locked gate on the dock leading to the ship; I am wondering if this is just Brazilian bureaucracy or there is a snafu! After some delay in the intense heat the gate opens, and my LEX-NATIONAL GEOGRAPHIC adventure is about to begin.

This my first sight of that amazing ship – the National Geographic Explorer – is exciting but at the same time intimidating. After dragging my considerable luggage up the gangplank (or is it the deck stairway?) it is all a bit confusing – everyone is gone but the ship's officers. The guests are ashore on an excursion to the same market I visited yesterday with Bruno. The Philippine male staff and locals are loading on supplies, all stacked in crates in the narrow passageway in front of my assigned room on the "Mud Deck, Deck B." I bruised my leg trying to get past them. Then I made the first rookie mistake, how to know? Down on the Mud Deck I searched for a dining room and ended up stumbling into the Philippine crew dining area on a lower deck where the rice, vegetable and meat dish was indeed unusual; they kindly pointed me to the ship crew's buffet. Then there was time for me to do a tour of the ship; it was a quick and overwhelming whirlwind tour by Mike Felden (naturalist, photographer and video expert) who does Brazil and Peru for LEX. (I walked the ship alone later and am just a bit more familiar, but not much. Maybe that is why I did a thorough photo tour later.)

I have a private room on the mud deck but share a bath with one of the naturalists, Richard White the Ornithologist and "bird man" for the trip. I saw him very little since he gets up early and goes up to the bridge for the birds. In the tiny room the only ventilation comes from vents in the ceiling and natural light from one small round porthole. I feel like an enlisted sailor in the Lindblad Navy. It's pretty basic. I believe there was a bit of Explorer "culture shock" going on.

My Room, Staff Quarters, the Mud Deck

Later in that first, hot afternoon (it's all a blur) I met and had a great talk with Ronaldo and Marcos, ISS Port people in Belém. They were on board fulfilling Brazilian customs requirements. Ronaldo spent one year as an American Field Service student in Blackfoot, Montana, next to Glacier Park (Keah and I were in that bleak town and got gas on our way to the East Glacier entrance some years back.) He loved it, taught all the Indian kids how to play soccer Brazilian style! Think for a moment of Brazilian tropics and Montana winters!

Later, it was all still a blur, it was perhaps at dinner that evening or the routine of lectures the next day that I gradually met the big-wigs, the major speakers aboard, and then the naturalists and staff whom I would learn to admire ever more the next few days.

A NOTE ON LOGISTICS OF GUEST SPECIAL SPEAKERS AND STAFF ON LEX TRIPS

LEX protocol, in a nutshell, at least as I understood it as the "rookie," was as follows: the first in charge was the Expedition Leader who made all the major decisions during the expedition. The EL probably started as a naturalist or naturalist-photographer and gradually worked his or her way to this position after many trips and experiences learning the ropes over the years. My first was Bud Lenhausen of long naturalist fame and off the ship distant "neighbor" in Fort Collins, Colorado.

Next was the AEL, the Assistant Expedition Leader, in my view, honestly, the "workhorse" of the expedition, in charge of all logistics for on shore excursions. During my inaugural trip this was Lucho Verdesoto, a naturalist of long Galápagos experience, who spent most of the time at his desk and computer in the staff work room, either on the Internet or ship telephone coordinating the upcoming shore excursions. And there were always surprises and headaches. I'm sure there were duties I did not know about, but one important one was the traditional notice for embarkation procedures for both staff and guests. In effect this was the "nuts and bolts" aspect of what hopefully would be a smooth, uneventful expedition (Ha! They say).

The major number of LEX personnel then were the immensely qualified naturalists, oceanographers, photographers, undersea diving specialists, Medical Doctor, exercise-gym specialists, and in a few cases, the "culture" people like David Barnes, Ship Historian-Librarian, I as cultural specialist for Brazil, and on select trips, a ship pianist-musician. Of significant importance was the staff person in charge of arranging musical entertainment both on shore and at times on board, in our case the famous musicologist, entrepreneur and all around fantastic lecturer, Jacob Edgar of "Music Voyager" and "Putumayo" Productions. I'm probably leaving some important positions out. I'll introduce those I remember to you as time goes by.

What only became clear even into my second or third trip was that all the above personnel did far more than their main role, i.e. naturalist, photographer, diver, or the like. Some were "full-time" Lindblad employees spending up to half the calendar year on diverse ships and diverse expeditions to the far corners of the world. Many were contract employees signing on for specific trips according to need and expertise, i.e. the Bay of Baja California or the like. These people were also zodiac drivers, on-station emergency personnel, and they handled the graphics, sound, microphones and other needs for the presentations which were a vital part of the trip. I would see them doing early departure on the zodiacs to the docks (and at times the lack of docks) to greet the zodiacs with guests, help the latter manage the waves, surf and slippery steps on sometimes less than desirable landing conditions. And there was a lot I did not see.

As I gradually learned (listen to the announcements by the EL or AEL on the ship intercom or just mainly "keep your eyes open"), we all helped "clear" the tables after Recap, and a main task was the staff handling of luggage of all arriving and departing passengers, more on this sometimes hilarious, seemingly chaotic and incredibly quick and efficient procedure as times go by. And staff provided the new brochures and magazines placed in each guest room at the start of each expedition.

What of course needs to be described, and more so as we travel, is the actual crew of the Explorer, Captain, Mates, Hotel Manager, Purser, and jobs I don't even know about. And of course, the necessary kitchen and dining staff, bar and bistro service, afternoon tea service as well as afternoon snacks on the back deck as well as food for Recap, all this as well as the cabin attendants and the all-important laundry room. And there were the engineers who tended to the engines, machinery, and the ship itself, denizens of the depths of the ship, all important but especially so when there was a mechanical emergency or surprise! All this latter business as an amazing well-coordinated, efficient and pleasant thing was I guess to be expected in the LEX operation. I did not meet most of these people, but know many were from Germany, Sweden, Norway, and of course the Philippines in the case of cabin, dining and laundry crew.

The Explorer's normal guest capacity was about 170 passengers, a small group in comparison to the outlandish "cruise" ships known to most world travelers, but a perfect size for expeditionary travel. It took all the above people to make it work.

And finally, in this "nuts and bolts" overview of ship life, were what I like to call the "bigwigs," the special guest speakers for each trip, true experts in their fields brought aboard to provide an outstanding natural, cultural, and/or scientific experience. These people can be termed as "world experts" and I can say in my three expeditions, they never disappointed. I had my favorites to be sure, but all deserved to be aboard. I'll tell of encounters with them, and in my case, a truly humbling experience at one of the book signings. I think since I'm writing this book and am in charge here that I can say I was a "small fish in a big pond" yet as a "second tier" speaker did provide a needed and as it turns out, successful, contribution to the trips. Much more to be said of my experience as we go along, "the good, bad and the ugly."

WADE DAVIS

It was shortly after boarding, the first evening dinner and entertainment, and the following "day at sea" and ship routine, that I met Wade Davis who wrote a famous Amazon River book about the search by his Harvard mentor for the origin of the coca plant (he chewed coca leaves in research and experimented with other assorted psychedelics, all part of the job). Little did I know of Wade's amazing background, intellectual pedigree and major books. It gradually began to sink in during his presentations and our personal conversations, but only a year later when I checked him out on Wikipedia did it finally sink in - He is famous! Wade is the major cultural speaker on this trip and I'll soon discover why, a duty he shared with equally famous Tom Lovejoy. Wade is in that rare air category of NATIONAL GEOGRAPHIC SOCIETY EXPLORER. I would only learn much later and gradually of the amazing company I was introduced to and keeping on this ship. When I learned, the reader would find out.

Wade Davis, the Speaker's Podium, the Explorer

TOM LOVEJOY

I met Tom Lovejoy of "World Wildlife Fund" and "The Nature" series. He came to Brazil first in 1965, so we are contemporaries and that helped a bit to "break the ice." Thomas was instrumental in the 1960s in CONVINCING the Brazilian government that they should try to preserve the Amazon! He later would be the founder of the Nature Series and instrumental in the WWF. And he deserves credit for first coining the research term "biological diversity." As a scholar and professor his present academic connection is George Mason University. Like Wade, you must look up Tom on Wikipedia to be blown away by the man, his life and his accomplishments!

Tom Lovejoy, the Speaker's Podium, the Explorer

BUD LENHAUSEN

I met Bud Lenhausen the LEX Expedition Leader for this trip. Originally from Alaska, his home is now Fort Collins. He has been with LEX-National Geographic since 1978 and has been all over the world, very business - like but friendly.

Bud Lenhausen, Expedition Leader, Sugar Loaf, Rio, 2013

David Barnes

David Barnes is from Wales and is a man of many tasks aboard Explorer - Librarian, Historian, and General Staff on LEX ships for five to six months per year. As I would get to know him better, as with the others, the more impressed I became! He shared with me that "We have a bit of an edge on the other staff, being Academics and with the resulting privileges." Well, maybe off the ship! David has been with LEX for over twenty years, has served as EL mainly on the trips around England, Scotland, the Hebrides and Europe, is an academic expert on his native home of Wales, but most impressive is the immense knowledge garnered by preparing and giving cultural and historic lectures around the world on the ships. His manner was pleasant, his sense of humor at times understated (oh, the British) and at times satiric. His asides reminded me a bit of those of W.C. Fields. And on a later trip I would discover he had a singing voice, in Welsh that is.

David Barnes, Speaker's Podium, the Explorer

Jen Martin

I met my "boss" from the original telephone interview in Mesa - Jen Martin - who was delightful. Her main duty is as chief personnel person at LEX for evaluating and hiring staff, but she still manages to be on the ships throughout the year, often as EL. Her first love is SE Asia and she is a true "hot-rodder" on the zodiacs. She is away from shore duty on this special trip to organize and "herd" all the speakers for this long voyage.

Jen Martin, EL, Naturalist and Staff Manager, LEX

DENNIS CORNEJO

Dennis Cornejo is a salty and humorous undersea diver and expert, originally from the U of A in Tucson. He did the wrap up today on plants of the Amazon. He is a really engaging speaker, sprawls on the floor or bounces around and is full of jokes. And Dennis incidentally "wired me up" with microphone for the presentations and guaranteed that all would go smoothly for the "rookie," microphone, images and the like in the lounge and lectures from the speaker's podium, "Circle of Truth." More on him when we have a chance to talk later.

Dennis Cornejo, Undersea Diver and Naturalist, the Explorer

DOUG GUALTIERI

Doug Gualtieri is an EL and Naturalist for LEX originally from Alaska and a favorite of mine for saying his favorite bird is the Dipper which we see frequently on the Pine River near our property outside of Durango, Colorado.

Doug Gualtieri, EL and Naturalist, LEX

JACOB EDGAR

This is Jacob Edgar, a delight; he loves music and sets up lectures on board and live shows for the Expedition. I learned he has his own music studio and recording studio in Vermont, sponsors new, young, world artists, and has a weekly TV show on world music featuring a different place each week. He will be extremely generous with me with his music and Power Point Presentations on Brazilian culture and music. I am once again in rare company. Tonight, Jacob has arranged for us to have a 75-year-old lady singer with her band from the state of Pará who will do "caboclo" or northern Brazil music. All listen and dance on the back deck as we leave Belém and Guarujá Bay; the evening weather on the water is delightful as we watch the lights of the city disappear and head to high sea.

Jacob Edgar, Musicologist, the Explorer

FIRST DINNER AND PASSENGERS, MY "BAPTISM"

That first dinner in the dining room for me on the Explorer was of course an introduction to a major aspect of any LEX trip. By and large, the tables seated perhaps eight guests; there were many smaller square tables that seated four or six. All looked out of the many windows to the sea. There was no assigned seating, so guests arrived and either sat by pre- arranged agreement with friends or just as likely at open tables. We as staff were expected to dine with the guests, making sure to get to know as many as possible, share conversation and answer any questions. In my case I had more questions of them than they of me, almost all were regular, repeating guests on the LEX trips around the world. There was one advantage curiously enough – my age! I was able to relate to many of the times and tales of the guests that we shared just in living experience, that plus the fact of my share of the "blarney" inherited by many of us Irish-Americans.

There is one staff note that I only picked up on much later – I think there was always a kind of informal "staff" daily meeting during the breakfast hour – this I can only surmise for planning and coordinating the day's activities and shared tasks. I noticed many of the staff sitting together outside the dining room, in the bistro area at breakfast time. I rarely joined them, not to avoid them, but thinking my primary duty was to be with the guests during meals. Was I wrong? As will be mentioned, the fact I was new, indeed part-time help, I think kept me from participating more in what I later perceived as the "old-timers'" custom.

I will talk of the food on board but not in detail now, first because as the son of small town farm folks in Abilene, Kansas, I did not share the "fine dining" gourmet food experience of many, but I think they were greatly pleased. In fact, guests raved about the cuisine! I will share, within the guidelines of privacy by LEX for their guests, anecdotes of some conversations, but never names or photos. In my opinion, with due permissions of course, the latter would have added an entirely different dimension to this book. So be it.

Breakfast was always tasty, served buffet style, guests eating at the same tables already mentioned. An array of breads, cereals, yogurt and breakfast desserts was available as were juices, milk, and such. The buffet line featured eggs, breakfast meats, potatoes, and fruit. I am sure I am leaving much out. There were choices for the "vegans" as well. At table, the waiting staff provided hot coffee, other drinks and always efficient service.

Lunch was buffet as well, often served within the parameters of a.m. and p.m. shore excursions. A menu was placed on one of the shelves as you entered the buffet. It always featured salads, various cuts of meat, vegetables, potatoes, rice or such, fish in different sauces, and the like. Once again there were several dessert choices. Soft drinks, ice tea, or if you chose, wine or beer could be ordered, but I noticed that the p.m. schedule pretty much precluded alcohol intake for most.

Dinner was indeed "fine dining," with a menu or "cardápio" as we say in Brazilian Portuguese offering three choices of appetizer, main dish, dessert and the like. Many guests kept their own wines chosen beforehand from the wine cellar, but one could always simply ask for a glass of wine or a beer, and of course soft drinks, tea and the like. The desserts were special and a highlight. One could of course if especially ravenous add to the menu.

One should recall, and I will talk of this, that the 4:00 p.m. tea with its delicacies, surprise treats from the barbecue on the back deck and the snacks during Recap added to the pleasure. An open bar with spirits, wine or beer during that time preceded the dinner hour.

This introduction all brings me to my first dinner in the "formal" dining room aboard Explorer. I sat with a lady guest who has an M.S. in Spanish and is originally from Memphis; we had much to talk about. At the table was a male guest, humorous, who shared with me a love for Gary Larson cartoons.

We had lox, grilled rack of lamb and "cafezinho" for that first "fine dining" meal. I thought, "If it is all going to be like this, amazing."

On that first night, I recall the guests comparing how many trips they had done with LEX and where. Amongst them were many serious birders and/or photographers. One of the reasons they were aboard was to be enrolled in the expedition course led by the famous National Geographic photographers – David Colthrane, Tyrone Taylor, David Wright, Cotton Coulson and Sisse Brimberg of Sweden.

There was news at table that first night – LEX is cutting the Salvador stay to one day, starting the evening of arrival with the Ilhé Ayé music and drums. The emphasis on the trip is NATURE, culture is second. As expected.

FIRST NIGHT ABOARD ROCKING WITH THE WAVES

Thursday, October 4.

On that first night, I slept poorly; the ship rocked with sounds like "Master and Commander" except it was not rigging from the wooden deck and masts in the film but the wooden cabinets in my room on the mud deck. I am sleeping on the bottom bunk of a staff quarters room. The bunk above has about a two - inch shelf facing the aisle; I put my hearing aids on that top bunk the first night thinking all was well. The rock and roll of the ship knocked them off during the night. It was panic time; the next morning I searched every nook and cranny of that room, down on hands and knees, for the damned hearing aids. No luck and desperate, I saw the little Philippine cabin attendant cleaning the rooms, told of my predicament and asked her please to look around. Later, after attending talks upstairs, I came back, saw her and she with a big smile on her face, said "You were looking for these"? She found one on the bunk, one on the floor. Needless to say, the aids were placed in their travel case in my suitcase from that time on! I don't know if we need to keep track, but perhaps this was "rookie" mistake number one.

An aside: When water is rough on Explorer they extend rope guides throughout the public areas to hang on to, so no one falls. Anti-seasickness pills are available on the main counter before heading into the dining room. I took them twice, had no problems other than feeling a bit queasy.

NEXT MORNING October 5th

I had breakfast with wonderfully interesting guests. He does research on enzymes, HIV research, and is a very high-powered professor at one of the major state universities. His wife is a psychiatrist. He talked at length of research funding; his remarks sounded much like similar ASU research funding problems from my days.

There was no time to be outside and miss the spectacular speakers and talks, so no outside photos yet.

RICHARD WHITE

At about this time I met my "roomie," ever so briefly, Richard White, on full – time LEX-NG staff as ornithologist. He spent most of the trip either on the bridge or on the bow watching for birds, whales, etc. That day he gave a talk "Birds of the South Atlantic to Ascension Island in mid Atlantic." I remember highlights dealing with turtles and eggs. He is from the UK, has a 4,500-bird list (of 9000 on the planet!). He was a busy, serious fellow except for his formal presentations. His reputation precedes him: a world expert!

CURRAN'S FIRST TALK

An Aside: Just before the talk there is an email from Trafford Publishing Company: my book "Portrait of Brazil in the 20th Century – the Universe of the 'Literatura de Cordel'" is live! I am a happy camper and sent a note to wife Keah with the news.

So, I was the "rookie" on this expedition and they wanted to "check me out." I wrote to Keah afterwards, "Keah, it went phenomenally well! I doubt that any talk I ever gave at a university conference, anytime, received more compliments. There was a lot of humor and they loved the Portuguese jokes. The naturalists and photographers came up and said I was a terrific addition to the program. They loved it, 5 stars."

The round speaker's podium in the center of the lounge where all the talks are given is called the "Circle of Truth." Most of the staff veterans bring a small laptop, put it on the counter, and control images from that, and they prefer to hold the microphone in one hand. I, new to all this, brought the images on a flash drive which was loaded into the ship system (I was warned later that that can cause all kinds of trouble with viruses or your material disappearing into the void), and was "wired" with the lapel mike, a good thing. The ship was rolling in rough sea when I gave the talk, so I stood much of the time outside the podium and leaned on one of the nearby columns for support. And besides, I like to use my hands when I talk. Since this is my work and I own the copyright the reader sees the summary.

Mark Curran. Speaker's Podium, the Explorer

CURRAN: AN INTRODUCTION TO BRAZIL

    I.   The Brazilians and a Glance into the Brazilian Character

a. "El español es lindo; o português é bacana."
b. "A loura suada" [the sweaty blonde]. "Sem bigode" [no mustache]. "Sem colarinho" [no collar please]. All terms for "Choppe" draft beer. Good brewmeisters (all Nazi refugees goes the national joke).
c. Land of the future; always was; always will be (and is in 2013).
d. Revolution of 1964 – Tanks on Avenida Atlântica in Rio de Janeiro; traffic jam on the beach; a bit of a bother.
e. "O jeito." "Somos comodistas, não comunistas" Avoid bloodshed; a lack of violence is a national stereotype; it has all changed.
f. "Apareça." Come on by and see me sometime.
g. "Buttons." The question of physical distance during conversation.
h. Snapshot: painting the national library.
i. Snapshot: adjusting the mirror on the driver's side of the bus … with the gearshift.
j. "Peba. Peba."

II.   Brazil: An Introduction

Size/ population/ "they speak Portuguese"

The Brazilian mosaic – Portuguese, African, German, Italian, Native Indian, Japanese, and yes from American Civil War

The land: desert/ rich farm land/ plantation economy/ savannah/ jungle

National hyperbole: language most difficult/ best looking women/ richest resources / industrialization, globalization n. 1 in the world with several products

Swim attire: maiô/ bikini/ tanga/ fio dental [dental floss]

Religion: Catholic, Nominal Catholic, African religion (candomblé), Umbanda, Kardec Spiritist, Protestant, Jewish, Mormon

Carnaval, Land of !

Today's problems: rich-poor/ drugs/ violence, hunger but there is good news: oil, lots of land and good land, hardworking people

History: Blame it on Portugal (Portuguese jokes)

Flexible Character, mixture of race

White, black, and all others (160 categories once upon a time)

An Aside. All seemed amazed at my facility in Portuguese ("That's funny. You don't look Brazilian!") There was one critique by one person: my first talk was not up-to-date. "Explain this more," one says. My defense: it was not supposed to be "up to date" but an historic introduction.

The talk was followed by lunch with guests who talked of the Portuguese immigrants on the East Coast of the U.S. and the old whaling industry in New England.

TALK WITH TOM LOVEJOY

Then there was a "must" talk from Tom Lovejoy, a real "heavy weight" from Washington, D.C., founder of the Public Television Series "Nature" and inventor of the term "biological diversity." He was calm, methodical and spoke of important ecological issues especially in the Amazon. (I mentioned him in my next talk, a good first collegial move.) He is known to have been the single person responsible for getting the Brazilians and the Brazilian government to protect the Amazon! He spends most of his time working for such causes in Washington, D.C. and is a Professor at George Mason University as well.

RODRIGO MOTERANI – SHIP VIDEOGRAPHER

The expedition videographer is a mainstay on all LEX trips. He documents on film the major events of the trip, including moments on board but especially the on-shore excursions. The video is then made available to guests and staff at the end of the journey, a terrific souvenir of the trip often shared by guests with family or friends who become prospective travelers with LEX. Rodrigo enters the story several times the next three weeks.

Rodrigo Moterani is a Brazilian from Belo Horizonte and knows his country well. He has lived the past few years in Ecuador and has been on the LEX trips to the Galápagos. I was "selected" by videographer Rodrigo to do a video introduction for Fernando de Noronha. He supplied some information which I must memorize before we arrive at the archipelago. I came to know that this is indeed standard procedure on the trips. Staff are called upon for diverse moments in the trip, and the duty is shared by all. The fly in the ointment is that one is not necessarily sharing areas of expertise but must research (in the staff office, on the computers and Internet) the new topics. I'll write more of this and more so in later trips; my short contributions in 2013 were not exactly Academy Awards moments.

TYRONE TURNER NATIONAL GEOGREAPHIC PHOTOGRAPHER

I had great rapport with Tyrone Turner, a free-lance photographer on board by National Geographic, his first trip with Lindblad. He spent two years in Brazil's Northeast. We really got on great! A wonderful kid. He comes into the story later.

Dinner that night was with the same Tyrone and a wonderful lady, a Brazilian living in the U.S. I took it as a compliment that she agreed with all the points of my first talk. The conversation was in Portuguese. The food: steak in sauce, lobster with noodles, ice cream with chocolate sauce. The lunch that day was buffet: chicken, noodles, ice cream and chocolate sauce. And great café espresso!

It was overwhelming to meet and try to remember all the guests' names, all 138 of them, but it is a staff duty to be with them, socialize at meals, and answer any questions. And for many reasons we had great rapport, perhaps my age and ability to tell some tales part of the reason.

DAVID WRIGHT – EMMY AWARD WINNING PHOTOGRAPHER

Tonight I met David Wright, yet another of the National Geographic photographers aboard (LEX had loaded the ship with such folks for the 125th anniversary trip) with two Emmys for his nature films on a series for National Geographic ("Planet Earth"): Mountains/ Deserts/ Seas! Phenomenal. Clever. We would get along well. An aside: he was a Vegan along with Cotton Coulson. I noticed they ate beans and other "grazings" for breakfast. Just one example of his terrific work will be seen in his presentation on black bears in the forests of Minnesota.

David Wright, Emmy Winning Photographer, Cacao Plantation, Ilhéus

TOM RITCHIE, COTTON COULSON, SISSE BRIMBERG, DAVID COTHRANE –
NATIONAL GEOGRAPHIC PHOTOGRAPHERS

As time passed, more of the staff came up, introduced themselves and offered to help, "Just ask
for it." The "biggies" come up and introduce themselves, but it is hard to remember all the
names. Tom Richie (long-time naturalist with LEX, often Expedition Leader, does Antarctica,
the Arctic and others), Cotton Coulson (photographer on staff with National Geographic),
married to Sisse Brimberg. (Cotton will die in a tragic diving accident two years after this trip, a
sad occasion especially for wife Sisse but really for the entire LEX organization. Cotton had
been a mainstay on the expeditions for years).

There is news from Bud Lenhausen, Expedition Leader: at Fernando de Noronha I am assigned
"History on Shore," (I had hoped to do the hike in the forest and see the famous dolphins and
snorkel. Fortunately, this came to pass the second day at Noronha.) This is an appropriate time
to inform the reader that one of the main reasons I decided to sign on to this and subsequent trips
with LEX-NATIONAL GEO was precisely to get a chance to see in Brazil and other places the
very aspect I had not seen before: Nature! (It was not a priority in prior research trips.) It did not
happen and there was no mystery why: I was signed on as a "Cultural Speaker" and therefore
was expected to always accompany any excursion that smacked of local history or culture. While
naturalists and guests hiked and hunted for birds, I was at old forts and the like. It makes sense:
Curran would not be too good at pointing out "that yellow and black bird" over there in the
underbrush! But it took me a while to realize it. I did indeed keep my eyes open and camera
ready and there were a few "accidental" moments when wonderful birds, marmosets, capybaras
and the like appeared in front of the lens of my "not up to snuff" expedition camera. One major
case to be seen was the opportunity to join the naturalists at the Chico Mendes TAIM reserve in
Rio Grande do Sul, Brazil.

THE EXPLORER GIFT SHOP

Explorer has a wonderful gift shopped manned by Andrew a veteran of many years with LEX. There is all manner of very high-quality souvenirs – ship clothing with logo, jewelry, National Geographic Society souvenirs and the like. I bought my first gifts in the gift shop: Explorer baseball caps, Explorer stocking caps, all for gifts.

The gift shop also offers books, thus my humbling story and Andrew's application of how to make lemonade if they give you lemons. Already mentioned is the reason I was even invited to join Explorer for this trip was a retirement book "Adventures of a 'Gringo' Researcher in Brazil in the 1960s – In Search of the "Literatura de Cordel." Andrew, being his efficient self, had ordered who knows how many copies to be brought on board (for a book signing later in the trip). And the book was announced to guests prior to the trip and I understand several were sold. So far so good. At the end of the story, or the trip in 2013, many copies were left, and Andrew approached me saying, "Since you may not be on board again, please sign these copies for probable future guests." Gulp! Those were sobering words; I spent a hurried 30 minutes signing books before leaving the ship. The story has a happy ending since unknown at that time I would be on board for two additional trips, but I doubt that all the books were ever sold. The book signing afternoon is quite another story, a memorable and humbling moment for yours truly. My only defense of the latter is that since 2013 many writing projects have come to fruition, perhaps further justifying presence on the ship.

It was one unforgettable moment, truly a humbling experience, when the ship intercom announced a "book signing" party outside the gift shop on the main deck of the Explorer. Dutifully following the instructions of Andrew, Gift Shop Director, I found a seat, one among three, in front of the shop on a given afternoon. Wade Davis, Tom Lovejoy and myself were to be available to guests to sell and sign our books. All I recall is one-half hour sitting quietly watching person after person come up to Wade and Tom, praising their works and lives, and me much like a fly on the wall during the time. In retrospect, and in all honesty, perhaps one or two persons asked about me and my book, but looking back on the experience, I can only say how I was blessed and to be, even momentarily, in the presence of such scholars and human beings. I shall always remember the moment.

The Gift Shop, the Explorer

SHIP LOGISTICS – LAUNDRY ON THE EXPLORER

The laundry system for staff: they leave a laundry bag in your room; you take it to the laundry room, whenever, each day generally, and they return (or you pick up) in 24 hours. The laundry is down the hall of B deck where we are bunked. It worked out well. The Philippine staff does all laundry, assisting in the galley and waiting at tables. The hot, huge laundry room was down the way from staff cabins and office.

RECAP TONIGHT

I experienced my first "Recap," already explained in the introduction to "Recap" on the Explorer and other LEX expedition ships. This is where the naturalists shine, first in what they saw that day, but in addition incredibly entertaining and informative short vignettes on nature throughout the planet.

Recap tonight was great fun! Richard White did "futebol," Tom Richie did "Sloths," and Dennis Cornejo did "Amazon." Funny and salty.

Incidentally another "custom" on board is "Afternoon Tea" at the Bistro on the same deck as the dining room. I personally did not take part most days simply due to the large lunch and the upcoming snacks at Recap and then dinner. Today there were four kinds of Amazon ice creams at 4 p.m. It all takes some personal planning. Guests must balance needs and desires and seem to have no difficulty in the task.

At night, I still noted the balancing of the ship in the waves and the sound like the groaning of the rigging in "Master and Commander."

MEETING MORE GUESTS

I met a lady whose husband worked in Macapá in far Northern Brazil and then the famous Ipanema, its opposite in Rio de Janeiro. Then there was a wonderfully alive lady and elderly husband. She was my favorite, reminded me of my wife Keah's grandmother Nanny in Little Rock, a livewire and clever and a bit sarcastic. She would sit beside me on the bus to the "Estancia," in Uruguay livening the trip.

Then I met a guest from THE Ohio State University (as he gently reminded me); he is a single on the trip and is a big-time birder. He kept me up to date with football scores, i.e. Notre Dame 37, ASU 34. I write every now and again of the Jesuit University pedigree and then a career teaching at Arizona State University, often feeling, I guess, a need to justify the latter in such elevated company on the ship. Once again, check my web page; the defense rests.

AT SEA October 5th

A.M. David Cothrane, Tyrone Turner, and Sisse Brimberg gave talks on photography. This is part of the photo instruction program for guests, an extremely popular and important part of the Expedition. One cannot find more qualified or experienced photo instructors.

11 A.M. FIRST WADE DAVID TALK: "INTO THE SILENCE"

Wade Davis gives the talk based on his magnificent book "Into the Silence," the story of trench warfare in WW I, both for upper class Brits and commoners, with horrible scenes of warfare, deaths, crippling injuries, and the survivors to Everest. Mallory was the head. It was like Wade had an elaborate, elegant, literary text memorized! It turns out he has been doing this since 1981 so that may be so. I thought, "He is the best speaker I have ever heard, bar none!" And I told him so. They say he is LEX – NATIONAL GEOGRAPHIC's number one speaker! He does around-the-world jet tours as well. Check out his book on the Amazon and his Bio. If you Google him it is amazing.

After Wade's talk I had the opportunity to have cafezinho with Wade and Jacob Edgar. It was a great conversation and moment. That would continue …

LUNCH WITH JACOB EDGAR AND JEN MARTIN

Lunch with Jacob and Jen Martin. As mentioned, she was asked to come aboard this trip to handle all the presenters and the talks via spreadsheet. She took notes while we did our presentations! But she managed later to zoom us around on the zodiacs!

P.M. JACOB EDGAR'S TALK: "INTRODUCTION TO BRAZILIAN MUSIC"

College at Oberlin; one-year backpacking and playing his guitar around the world. He did Latin American Studies but did not like Academia. Ended with Putumayo Records and travels the world looking for current or contemporary music. (And he does his own program, "Music Voyager" for PBS). He has a house, wife and kids in Vermont and a studio there. His talks for me were one of the real highlights of the presentation aspect of the trip – wonderful introductions to Brazilian music, especially the samba and to Brazil's great northeastern dance music of the "forró." And he was gracious, sharing the Power Points of all with me. Thanks again Jacob.

Jacob Edgar, Speaker's Podium, the Explorer

P.M. DAVID BARNES: "DARWIN AND THE 'BEAGLE'"

That same p.m. more good stuff kept coming. David Barnes, from Wales and a specialist on its culture including Darwin, did his talk on "Darwin and the 'Beagle'" to South America in 1832. Good, informative.

Miscellanea that p.m.

There was no recap but instead "caipirinhas" on the back deck and Amazon fish tacos or sausage tacos. So much tasty food and dinner yet to come! Incidentally the "caipirinha" is the Brazilian national cocktail. It begins with squeezing a huge bowl of limes, adding lots of ice, a bottle or two of Brazilian sugar cane rum ("cachaça") and more sugar than you've ever seen. The result is delicious and varies from one part of the country to another, but the other result may be indicated by a friend's very accurate description, "a rubber hammer!" It was a huge favorite at student parties over the years in Brazil. Cheap and enjoyable.

During dinner I picked up the staff guitar (kept in the dining room when the Philippine staff does the birthday songs) and sang "Mañanitas" for Jim Kelley's birthday. That "old guitar" (recall John Denver's song) would be part of the musical story of Explorer trips to come.

MORE SHIP LOGISTICS: COMPUTERS AND THE INTERNET

On this trip I am introduced to and use the guest room computer for personal emails and for this diary. You purchase a card for $20 and mine lasted the trip. It turns out most guests have their own laptops or I-Pads and do not require the use of the room. I would learn and do the same in 2016. For ship work, presentations and the Daily Expedition Report (DER to come) the solution was the staff office on B Deck and the computers there.

AT SEA, ANOTHER DAY October 6th

TOM RITCHIE'S TALK ON "QUININE"

Up and breakfast with guests and Tom Richie. He later gave a talk on "Quinine," the Indian Bark "quinoa." The Jesuit missionaries discovered it; Tom told the whole story and variants. Two Michelin Stars! Great.

TOM LOVEJOY'S SECOND TALK: "BRAZIL 1965-2013"

11:00 a.m. Tom Lovejoy, anecdotes from 1965 to 2013. A researcher, now an executive in D.C., instrumental in convincing Brazil to start saving the Amazon. And university professor. His base is D.C. for job – funding for World Wildlife Fund, etc. and "Nature" on PBS. There was a plethora of names telling the story of the people involved in the Amazon odyssey. Tom was kind to me; we shared jokes, and are contemporaries, but Yale did come up now and again. I do not know if this was in any way related to ASU. A calm speaker, deliberate, good, effective.

MARK CURRAN'S SECOND TALK: "BRAZILIAN CULTURE – INTRODUCTION AND A THUMBNAIL SKETCH"

How to get a grip on it? Google anything of interest: Wikipedia or Britannica.

Brazil by its regions. Charles Wagley. Introduction to Brazil. Cultural Anthropology. 1960s.

An Update on Brazil. Joseph Page. The Brazilians. 1990s.

A More Recent Update: Brazil.   Larry Rohter. Brazil on the Rise. 2013.

Politics: Thomas Skidmore

History: E. Bradford Burns

History from popular literature: Curran. "A Portrait of Twentieth Century Brazil – the Universe of the "Literatura de Cordel."

I.   It started with Portugal and the Portuguese

A. Language. Contrast Portugal and Brazilian (the Brazil Club T-Shirt). In the U.S. we say "uhhh;" in Mexico: "este"; in Brazil "pois," but in Portugal it's "cãã." "RR" is trilled in southern Brazil, on TV, but otherwise aspirated: "h."

B. Religion - Roman Catholic and the rest
African Spiritism
Kardec Spiritism
Protestants, Jews, Mormons, Native Spiritism

C. Architecture – highlights only
1. The "Brazilian Baroque:" Bahia and its churches/ Olinda and Recife/ Ouro Preto/ Congonhas/ The Igreja da Glória and Mosteiro de São Bento in Rio.
2. The 19th and Neo-Classical. Candelaria and "Teatro Municipal" and National Library in Rio (painting the national library). Public buildings in São Paulo.
3. 20th century: New - São Paulo's "Edifício Copan", the modern in "Pampulha" in Belo Horizonte and Brasília. Brasília: Oscar Niemeyer, Lúcio Costa.

D. Race: 160 classifications. White, Black, "Pardo," "Caboclo," "Mulato," Asian.

E. Carnival. History and Description. Rio de Janeiro, Bahia, Recife, São Paulo, etc. (My experiences Rio 1967: 10 days seeing it all with friends; National "guests" were Jorginho Guinle, Gina Lollobrigida and Brigitte Bardot). All the clichés: 3 days' vacation; dreams of the poor, freedom. Numbers' racket; today's glitz and sex and skin. Satellite TV to the world.

F. Cuisine – the food. The "gringo" with the fragile stomach. "Canja de galinha," stories of warm "gerimum," "mel de açúcar e farofa; sarapatel, comida Baiana." Portuguese: "bacalhau, lulas" and Fado Music.
African: "azeite de dendê, cocada, abaré, acarajé, xinxim de galinha, moqueca de peixe, caruru."
Feijoada in Rio with Black beans. It tastes terrific going down.
Gaúcho: "churrasco"
Northeast Interior: "feijão mulato, charque, farofa, rapadura, peixe, sarapatel"
Amazon Region – "açaí, pato no tucupi, peixe"
Italian/ German/ Jewish and more
Fish – meat – vegetables – Brazil can grow anything!

G. The Visual Arts (Google any of these terms.)

1. Painting: Anita Malfaldi, Cândido Portinari, Di Cavalcanti; MASP in SP
2. Sculpture: Aleijadinho in Ouro Preto and Congonhas do Campo
3. Landscaping: Roberto Burle Marx (Curran went to the beach.)

H. Literature. Padre Anchieta, Gregório de Matos, Castro Alves, José de Alencar, Machado de Assis Euclides da Cunha, Semana de Arte Moderna em São Paulo,

Mário de Andrade, Carlos Drummond de Andrade, Gilberto, Freyre, Romancistas do Nordeste (Graciliano Ramos, José Lins do Rego, Jorge Amado Raquel de Queiróz), Érico Veríssimo, Dias Gomes, Clarice Lispector, João Guimarães Rosa, João Cabral de Melo Neto, Ariano Suassuna (Curran's favorite: Luís Fernando Veríssimo and his Chronicles). But Brazilians complain that "nobody reads."

Cultural Institutions: Brazilian Academy of Letters, National Library (and the painting thereof), Museum of Art of São Paulo, Dom Pedro II Museum in Petrópolis, State of São Paulo Symphony; the Universities: NE, Rio, São Paulo

I. Folklore: Dances, Festivals, etc." Curran's special interest: "literatura de cordel."

J. Sports: "futebol." In Curran's "Adventures" see the Carioca championship, and then, Pelé and Santos at the Maracanã. Larry Rohter describes it well in 2013.

K. Popular culture-mass culture. The "Telenovelas." Priests changed the hour of mass in parts of Brazil. Glória Pérez, daughter Daniella: life imitates the "novela."

L. Performing artists – music. Jacob Edgar's expertise once again.
Heitor Villa Lobos / Dorival Caymmi/João Gilberto/ Antônio Carlos Jobim/ Chico Buarque de Holanda/ /Jair Rodrigues/ Nara Leão/ Vinicius de Morais/ Roberto Carlos/ Sertanejo music – seresteiros/ Axé/ Pagode/ Caetano Veloso e Tropicália/ all the samba/ folk: milonga from Rio Grande do Sul/ "cantoria" from Northeast.

M. Theater: 19th Century Romantic (plus a bit of opera); Nelson Rodrigues/ Dias Gomes/ Ariano Suassuna. Icons and Carnival.

N. Cinema: "Black Orpheus!"/ "Cinema Novo" and Glauber Rocha/ Fernanda Montenegro/ The Barreto Family Producers and cinema based on literary works. (Jorge Amado)

O. The Press: Diário de Pernambuco/ "A Tarde" in Bahia/ O Globo/ Jornal do Brasil/ Estado de São Paulo/ Folha de São Paulo/.
Magazines: Manchete/ Veja/ Época/ Isto É.
And one that ran into trouble: "Tribuna da Imprensa" and last days of General - President Castelo Branco 1967.

For all those left out, "sinto muito," a nearly impossible task. Maybe you will remember the anecdotes. "Obrigado." Mark Curran

FIRST TIME TO THE CHART DECK

By its name this is the public space where guests can view maps of the ship's progress, always helpful and interesting. The deck is also where there are large insulated mugs and coffee throughout the day. If you opened a drawer or two you might find some cookies as well; I was late in discovering the latter but evidently staff and guests knew of it.

It took a while, perhaps even on voyage two or three that I developed a comfortable a.m. routine of going to the Chart Room first for a hot mug of coffee and then to the bistro to sample their "early risers' breakfast" of fruit, cookies and perhaps a chocolate pastry. All this was found next to the healthy bowl of apples always available.

All this is being reported on Expedition I in 2013 when the process of exploring the ship brought me for the first time to the chart deck and then to the top captain's deck or bridge where I took photos and used ship binoculars and saw masked boobies and terns. Then I discovered a spot on my tiny, Sure Shot "old" camera; David Cothrane graciously agreed to look at it, fix if possible and I'll pick it up tomorrow. His later advice: after closing the lens and turning the camera off, tap on palm of hand, if this happens again. Photos of the chart room and maps of our progress:

The Chart Room, Explorer

RODRIGO MOTERANI – VIDEO CHRONICLE OF THE EXPEDITION, PART I

During that busy day there were more presentations to inform and entertain us. And these were followed by a presentation by Videographer Rodrigo, including all prior to my joining the ship at Belém do Pará. It was a presentation of the Video Chronicle of the first half of the trip by Rodrigo for all in the lounge. I saw all I had missed prior to getting on, and with mixed emotions – I missed some monkeys and pink Ibis in Trinidad-Tobago park, some birds, the Hindu Temple and the Synagogue in Paramaribo. The highlight was flocks of Pink Ibis in Trinidad, these were featured on the cover of the brochure for the trip. At the end of the trip I was able to get a staff copy of the final video, a wonderful souvenir.

THE CLIMATE CHANGE PANEL

Superb. The participants are world experts. Jim Kelley, renowned geologist and oceanographer advocates for climate change saying we don't worry how or why, just deal with it. Man must adapt, and he argues that scientific models must guide. Some of the scientist - guests debated it all with the panel. Tom Lovejoy: a scientist-politician participated. Wade Davis was the moderator. Suffice to say, with Wade Davis, Jim Kelley and Thomas Lovejoy's experience, this was an informed and stimulating discussion, the kind of thing LEX is good at doing.

POTPOURRI OF THE REST OF THE DAY

There were snacks and socializing on the back deck with Tyrone, Wade and David Wright. I basically just try to look on. Keep my ears open.

Dinner. With military man from Viet Nam days. Tired. To bed.

There was also talk that day with my birder guest from THE Ohio State University; he would keep me informed of the ASU – Notre Dame football results.

Later that day, probably during Recap and cocktails, there was an enjoyable conversation with a guest couple. In the mid -1960s he was on R and R in Recife, on leave from putting up communication towers on Ascension Island. He led the bachelor life in Recife and recognized some of my hangouts from those days on Boa Viagem beach. He related very much to my talks on the Northeast and we had shared some experiences. He would buy "Adventures" and like it. They became familiar faces and friends on the rest of the trip.

NEXT DAY, ARRIVAL AND STAY AT FERNANDO DE NORONHA October 7th

INTRODUCTIONN TO FERNANDO DE NORONHA

This was one of the highlights of the "Epic South America Expedition" due in part to the fact that the archipelago of Fernando de Noronha is a World Heritage Site by UNESCO due to its environment. There are 21 islands in the archipelago but the largest which we visited contains 91 per cent of the land. It is located due east of the Brazilian mainland but is administered by special arrangement with the State of Pernambuco. Later in the middle of the Atlantic on Trip II we shall see the famous St. Peter and Paul Rocks, literally that, also under Pernambuco administration. Oddly enough there is a research relation to my interest in Brazilian Northeastern Politics on Noronha.

I had to "study up" on all this with the unexpected request by videographer Rodrigo for me to talk of the historic forts on the Island. So, much time was spent on the computers in the Staff Office prior to arrival.

The islands were perhaps discovered as early as 1503 on a voyage that would continue to the Brazilian mainland, but interesting because of one of the passengers – Amerigo Vespucci. I say "perhaps" because there are at least four other versions. Nonetheless the archipelago during the next two hundred years became a collection point for goods from Brazil, including the famous Brazil Wood (a red wood used for red dye for clothing in Europe) and remained part of the Loronha family "Captaincy" during that time.

Captain Robert Fitz Roy of the "Beagle" fame came next in 1832 with orders from the crown to check the exact latitude and longitude of the place. His famous passenger, Darwin, admired the lush forest but was disappointed to not yet see hummingbirds, gaudy colored birds and flowers that he expected in the tropics.

In 1897 the Island became a prison, once again administered by the State of Pernambuco; it operated until 1957; Miguel de Arraes, Pernambuco president and suspected Leftist by the Brazilian Military was imprisoned there (he was a main topic in the "literatura de Cordel" of the 1960s).

In the 1940s Noronha's airport became part of the shuttle from Recife-Dakar in North Africa by the US Army-Air Force (flights from Natal and Recife to Noronha), and a military installation with cannon was built on the Island (LEX visited in 2013 and 2016). The original stone fort built by the Portuguese in the 17th century was also part of the tour.

Masked Boobies, Fernando de Noronha, 2013

In by Zodiac to Fernando de Noronha, 2013

THE TWO DAYS OF TOURING

I was up at 6:00 after a lousy night's sleep for the arrival at Fernando de Noronha. We are due to leave the ship at 8:30, it will mark my first zodiac ride EVER to a beach or dock. There is a Sailing-Yacht Regatta from Recife to Noronha, so the harbor is filled with $$$ sailing craft, strange for this "protected" area!

After the arrival by zodiac my group joined the van and the guide with limited English – we got on fine and I helped her translate some of her terms from Portuguese to English – to the top of the hill to the main Noronha town Vila dos Remédios. The group walked down a rough and steep cobblestone street to the Administration Building, the old prison administration building, saw the old cannons from WW II military installation, and on to the Vila church from the 1700s.

The World War II Cannon, Fernando de Noronha

After the modest church we all walked up to the old 17th century fort through pretty but dry forest; there were cannon abandoned, lying around, but there was a splendid view of the harbor. Saw a bit of the fort itself and then walked back downhill to the vans. It was incredibly hot and sticky. We had to get one of the guests under the cold air vent in the museum on the way to revive her.

After this initial excursion in the a.m. to the Fort, we got back on the bus, fortunately with a/c, to the port, and zodiac back to the ship. Shower. Lunch with David Barnes; I really liked him, Welsh, Brit, extremely clever, nice.

In the p.m. there is another excursion, this one with photos below. We were off once again at 1 p.m. on the zodiac, back to the docks and a "cruise," the "Dolphin-Snorkel Option." We saw zero dolphins (they do not keep the same schedule as our Excursions but would appear on the second time around the next day) some birds, beautiful water and beaches. The snorkeling: you jump in from the back of the boat; it was deep with a strong current. I swam over to the snorkeling area and alongside the big rock where the fish were supposed to be, but it was so deep I could not see fish well. This might be attributed in part to the fact I did not have a prescription snorkel goggle. (An aside: on the 2016 expedition I met the optician who came close to having the contract for such goggles with no less than Jacque Cousteau.) Most of the fish were on top of the rock. I was exhausted and had a slow, slow swim against the current back to the boat. I thought I might have to call for help but made it back, barely climbing back up the ladder. It was a bit of a scary experience. The water was cool and the current strong for me. Next day and next time around would be much better. Photos of that first foray follow.

Wade Davis, Photography, Fernando de Noronha

RECAP, FIRST DAY IN FERNANDO DE NORONHA – A CONVERSATION WITH WADE AND GAIL DAVIS

That evening during Recap and social hour I talked to Wade Davis's wife Gail and heard her advice (to me, an amateur classical guitarist) on fingernail care for classic guitar (she is a serious guitarist with concert capabilities and a fine instrument).

David Barnes did the wrap up, on Darwin and the Beagle. Richard White talked, showing only two birds from the day, but this was a good day (it turns out there are only two endemic birds on Noronha, one a vireo which we saw in 2016). Then Jacob Edgar did a short presentation on Paraíban music and "forró." I loved it.

Dinner with was with guests from Germany. Lamb loin, cuscus, black bread, wine, ice cream and chocolate.

A CONVERSATION WITH DAVID BARNES

I had a wonderful "off the record" talk with David Barnes. Such talks were one of the ways to learn the ropes on board as staff. David was positive toward me and my work and says I'm doing okay. He said next year's trip is only 17 days, Buenos Aires to Bahia. He explained that doing History for LEX is his strong suit. LEX runs the trip, National Geo adds its name, not necessarily passengers, but adds scholars, photographers, etc. David is on for six months during an average year, then home to Wales. Two months on and two off. He just did Africa, the Azores, Cabo Verde and the boat over to Brazil. It is a full-time job for him and significant as part of the total living plan. He develops talks on all regions of the world!

DAY TWO – FERNANDO DE NORONHA October 8th

The morning brings news to me: suddenly I am assigned on the morning excursion as "group leader" to the Fort at Fernando de Noronha; it will be a return trip for me.

There is talk of my participation in a possible recap assignment on the Rio Party house for the 125th Anniversary Gala, supposedly done by famous Brazilian architect Oscar Niemeyer. It would culminate a few days later combining a recap for Introduction to Rio plus the Niemeyer slides. All this only happened after some tension and difficulty getting stuff from the staff computer for this my first participation ever in Recap for LEX.

BUS CAPTAIN TO THE FORT

Up at 6:30, breakfast at 7:00, leave on zodiac for Fernando de Noronha dock and the fort. The van goes once again to Vila dos Remédios. David Cothrane, Tom Richie, Bud Lenhausen, Pete Poulson and David Wright were all along, an amazing gathering of people I would only appreciate much later. I am "group leader" but they helped out greatly with the duties of counting on the buses, seeing who would work "independent" and watch those who could not walk or keep up. I indeed did this latter duty, keeping track of a guest using a walker and with great difficulty on that cobblestone street; we managed to get her an early return to the zodiac and the ship. The Brazilian Michelle was our guide again. I explained in English some of her terms in Portuguese. There was time to really document the museum with its history of the Island, the forts and particularly the inmates of the prison.

The video interview was only "so-so" (recall it was also my rookie introduction to this aspect of LEX trips). Rodrigo wanted sound bites and the professor not talking so much. I said: "It's all your fault for all the information you gave me to memorize!" I recall his instructions: "Look this way, that way, blablabla." We both got a laugh out of it.

After that interview at the old fort on the top of the hill in terrific heat, we took the van back to port. There was good rapport with guide Michelle. I gave her my web page address and business card from ASU. I was soaked with sweat. Zodiac to the ship, shower. The "Swedish dessert" to die for: chocolate and coconut. Best on the trip! And to my chagrin never again! I was too naïve to ask for the recipe, the horse already out of the barn when I thought of it later.

The same day, in the p.m. it's back to the boat ride in the p.m. This time it turned out much better, in fact, great. We saw the spinning dolphins in the front wake of the tour boat. Lots of photos; did not think to do video. Remedied that later in the trip. Had much better snorkeling this time, wearing light vest, Trigger fish, Angel Fish, small colored fish, but did not see the Barracuda that others saw. The water was indeed gorgeous. Photos below.

Passing the Explorer on the Way to Snorkeling, Fernando de Noronha

A much happier Curran this second time around with improved dolphin sightings and snorkeling.

BACK TO THE SHIP – THE RESPITE

Back to the ship, shower, recap. Good talk with Wade and Gail Davis and Tyrone Turner.

The recap: Dennis Cornejo's underwater filming and deep dives and beautiful fish. Then Jacob' s music talk on Northeastern Brazilian music - "forró" with Luis Gonzaga singing "Asa Branca." ("White Wing" in a recent Russian documentary on Brazil was called "the Northeastern National Anthem.") Then EL Bud Lenhausen outlining plans for the coming days.

At dinner I was exhausted. With the Brazilian lady and Tyrone. Earlier had spent considerable time in the "staff office" printing notes for next talk.

ANOTHER ROOKIE MOMENT AND PRESSURE

Only one of my portable hard drives works; the ship system would not accept two others. So, I lucked out. The images for all the talks were on them. Curran efficiency meant three portable hard drives; as mentioned only one of the three was compatible with the ship's audio-visual setup.

AT SEA AFTER FERNANDO DE NORONHA October 9th

Up at 6 a.m., preparation and review for my talk.

CURRAN'S THIRD TALK: "RELIGION IN BRAZIL"

I gave my third talk - on religion - at 9:30. It went okay; David Barnes and Wade Davis both referred to it in their subsequent talks. No small compliment; first time there was use of images, went well. Here is the summary:

"Brazil – the world's largest Catholic Country." 150 million believers? A "nominal" Catholicism. About 72 per cent of Brazilians claim Catholicism today as opposed to 90 per -cent in the early 1970s. Why the change?

1. Competition within the church between Progressives and Conservatives
2. Increased competition from Evangelical Protestants like the "Igreja Universal do Reino de Deus." Universal Church of the Kingdom of God and spinoffs.
3. Continuing African-Brazilian spiritualists
4. Continuing Kardec spiritualists
5. Continuing Protestant evangelization from the United States: Assembly of God, "mainline" Protestant churches, Pentecostal churches and Mormons.

History of the Catholic Church in Brazil

1.The prestige of the European Catholic Church during discovery and colonization: they had defeated the Moors and thrown them out of Europe, and with "Royal Patronage," that is, the kings name the clergy, the effective union of Church and State.

2. "Flexible" Portuguese Catholicism: isolation of church in Brazil, distances, the priests needed a "family" so they made one; concubinage was common and "accepted."

3. Center of colonial life was the plantation with its chapel and not a traditional "parish." Priest was second in charge often on the plantation. Part of the power structure. Unmarried daughters often went to the "Convent.'

4. Role of the Jesuits. 16th and 17th centuries: missionary work amongst Indians, The "Reductions" or "Jesuit States" in the South near Paraguay ("The Mission" deals with this.) Tried to place Catholic values on the landholders. But the utopic missions lost out to the "Bandeirantes", gold and slave hunters. Jesuits were expelled for political motives in 1767 from Brazil and Latin America.

5. The Church accepted the concept of Negro slavery.

6. But Catholicism was a "veneer" for the slaves; "real" religion was maintained.

7. 19th Century; Brazil independent from Portugal and now an Empire (Dom Pedro I, II). The church was connected to the State, protected as the "official religion," but subordinate to the State. Dom Pedro II who was Catholic and Mason, distanced himself from the Church. Vatican condemned Masonry, Pedro refused, crisis, some imprisonments and result: separation of church and state in 1889 with the Republic and freedom of religion in Brazil. The Catholic church is weakened.

8. Religion fanaticism in the Northeast. The "Messianic" movements and Sebastianism. Superstition, mysticism, folk religion. Some results.

> Lack of priests, immensity of Brazil, little formal contact with Rome.

> Even priests in the annual "missions" to reach the people preached that the droughts were a result of sin and that faith, prayer would solve the problems.

> Pedra Bonita in Pernambuco State, 1836

> Messianic Movement: "Good Jesus" Antônio Conselheiro, War of Canudos 1896

> Padre Cicero. Juazeiro do Norte, Ceará State. 1880s to 1934. Miracles.

> Friar Damián: fire and damnation and condemnation of the modern

9. "Renaissance of the Church" in 1920s, 1930s, family and anti-communism.

"Aparecida" in Sao Paulo State. 1717 to Present, apparitions of the Virgin.

10. CNBB. National Council of Brazilian Bishops. 1950s, 1960s. Concerns: lack of social justice, in favor of agrarian reform, role of "Dom Hêlder Câmara" [he and Mother Teresa 1976, Philadelphia] The "red" bishop: house machine gunned by the para-military right in 1960s, 1970s. "Violence of hunger" Liberation Theology. [Curran meets in Recife]. The Catholic "left." Priests murdered; nuns, as well when allied with poor.

11. Reactions of the "right" to President Goulart's "base reforms" of the 1960s. "Tradition, Family and Property" Anti-left, anti-Communist, in favor of military.

12. 1964-1985. Military arrested and tortured leftist Catholics. But the church reacted and became the main force against dictatorship, the only institution that could protest the disappeared and dead without repercussion: the Military did not "dare."

13. The Church today: (see the introduction and concerns, p. 1)

Religion: the Other Brazil

1.African spiritism: Page estimates 1/3 of Brazilians participate in some way.

    Religious syncretism: "mixture" of religions"

    The "Orixás" or saints. Possession by the saint.

    Ritual, mythology, and customs.

    Xangô Recife

    Candomblé Bahia

    (Indian version of same: "Pajelança" in Amazon region)

2."Macumba," "Umbanda" and "Quimbanda" Rio, São Paulo

    Total mixture of Catholic, African, Eastern Mysticism.

    "Amorphous" or hard to define, pin down. Reincarnation, the "spirits"

    both Catholic and other. Magic may be involved, hexes in "Quimbanda."

3. Kardec Spiritism 1854 and today. Allen Kardec, France.

    Spiritism based on the Bible and reinterpreted, reincarnation, no heaven or hell, The person can better himself, but no going back. Spiritualist healing (Arigó) Chico Xavier – medium and "spirit" writing.

4.The Evangelicals

    Edir Macedo and Universal Church of the Kingdom of God

    (It is estimated that the Catholic Church loses 600 000 to his religious "wave" each year.) Use of media on massive scale, constant services, tithing, no alcohol or drugs. Street corner evangelizing, promise of economic success, exorcism as basis of faith. Self-betterment, discipline, hard work. Dynamic.

5. "Believers" ["Crentes"] and the Northeast

    Debates/ old church versus Protestant "invaders"

    "The vulture and the Protestant preacher" Story-poem in the "Cordel"

    Sugar cane rum and the Protestants

6. Role of John Paul II and the Catholic "renaissance" Father Rossi, charisms. Pope Francis in 2013.

FLY IN THE OINTMENT

For whatever reason, the original plan for me to do the Bahia introduction as a one-hour presentation was changed to a segment in "recap" before Bahia, so I had to learn log-in on the staff computer down in the office on the mud deck, how to get images from the internet, save to thumb drive, doing all the above for a recap on "capoeira" and "candomblé." That Staff Office at first was all "Greek" to me; the staff and naturalists all seemed very busy with their own stuff, but David Barnes did show me the ropes and gradually I felt a bit more comfortable. The basic explanation of all this was simple: I was part-time, kind of a hybrid person on staff, more in line with cultural presentations (kind of a second tier to Wade Davis and Thomas Lovejoy). My presentations were all prepared; what was totally new was anything to do with Recap. I learned later that it was "part of the job" and simply, to be learned.

A TALK WITH TYRONE TURNER

 Tyrone is on staff for this voyage for National Geo. He is from New Orleans, young, maybe 45, did a National Geographic Article on the "quilombos" of Brazil, places where former escaped slaves lived in the interior of the Northeast, using black and white photos. His talk was on the drug sniffers in Recife, garbage collectors ["cata lixos"] in the garbage dumps of Recife, and the religious pilgrimages ["romarias"] in Juazeiro do Norte, Ceará, land of Father Cícero. The guests really loved it and loved his stark photography. He has prize winning black and white photography and he has a big heart! He has asked for advice on Brazil (all seem to rely on or trust my Portuguese.)

STRESS

As mentioned, one of my portable hard drives will not work on the ship. The NG Explorer tech-expert tried it and says I must get the password I used originally in Mesa when I connected it to the computer there. It may be impossible. I'm spending all my time in the staff office on the computer.

Lunch. Then to the computer to work on the Recap. Missed my nap, so no rest. It was an ordeal to get ASU e-mail. I tried several addresses and finally succeeded in writing home.

The staff uses the staff office on the Mud Deck and the internet to prepare all their short talks; they get photos and text and use Power Point. They are "old-timers" and veterans at this.

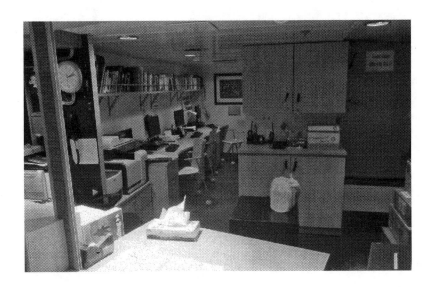

The Staff Internet Office, the Explorer

"THE ATLANTIC RAIN FOREST" TALK – DOUG GUALTIERI

Doug Gualtieri, one of the naturalists, is from Alaska and did the Atlantic Rain Forest talk. There is only something like 7 per cent left, yet it was and still is one of the most biologically diverse places on earth, much more than the Amazon. It was extremely informative and an eye-opener even for me, a veteran of Brazil.

"BRAZILIAN HISTORY" – DAVID BARNES

David Barnes did "Brazilian History," but it was more European and French. The talk was fine; he is well spoken, continental and all that, with a profound sense of humor.

I'm learning the ropes: being on staff you must ask questions. No one volunteers information; they are too busy, but if you ask they are happy to help. David Barnes gave tips and David Cothrane was an immense help; Richard White as well.

RECAP

Wade Davis did his talk on the Santo Daimé Religon in the Amazon and talked of the world's most powerful hallucinogenic drug, also called Santo Daimé, used in their rituals. The religion was begun by an African – Brazilian who had migrated from the State of Maranhão to the west

Amazon region of Acre during the rubber boom of the 1920s. It is called a "syncretic" religion because of the diverse sources which it uses (most familiar to me in research in Brazil): folk Catholicism, Kardec Spiritualism, African and Indigenous rituals as well. A major aspect is the use of "Ayahausca" a hallucinogenic drug from the Amazon used to produce visions and cathartic effects. Wade is an expert in such matters and I think he felt obligated for research to test the theses. An aside: As mentioned earlier, his wife Gail is a classical guitarist, a friend of Christopher Parkening, and will talk later of the value of good classical guitars, favoring Rosewood models from all over the world.

Wade was a bit critical of my expression of the "fear" I expressed in my talk on religion in Brazil, specifically in viewing my first Xangô ceremony in Recife. His view is that it is simply their religion and there should be no need to fear it, but rather respect it. Later he gave me a warm compliment after the Introduction to Bahia talk. I did the recap on "candomblé."

Doug Gualtieri did a short recap of his paintings of scenes of birds in Alaska.

He was followed by Dennis Cornejo who is a real jewel, a funny dive master with his commentary and beautiful film of fish seen at Fernando de Noronha. I did not see any of these in my snorkeling. Underwater folks dive with a long rod in their hand with the camera on the end; it gets into nooks and crannies.

DINNER WITH FUN GUESTS FROM FRANCE, AND DR. CARY, SHIP PHYSICIAN AND WIFE MIMI

Dinner with the French couple and ship doctor Dr. Cary and wife Mimi. The Frenchman is incredibly knowledgeable of the intricacies and delicacies of French cooking. He spoke of chocolate and white truffles which can produce a meal of one to two thousand dollars in a fine restaurant in Paris. And of course, he is a wine connoisseur. It was good to sit at his table because you get to try more than one kind and hear the comments.

THE "DONA FLOR AND HER TWO HUSBANDS" FILM

That night the "Dona Flor and Her Two Husbands" film was shown in the lounge, a classic from Brazilian cinema, based on one of Jorge Amado's best novels. Being the "Amado expert" on board, I of course was present, but it made for a late night. At first, I was disappointed at the crowd for there were very few people, but the "staff rookie" learned something new about the ship: you never know how many guests or staff are watching in their rooms. I discovered that all presentations, etc. can be seen on TV in the guests' rooms, so you never know who exactly listened to or saw your presentation. That night we talked in English, Portuguese and Spanish – the latter because Rodrigo, Paula and Alex from Ecuador were present, he on LEX staff for Galapagos (they are using the reduced fare system for LEX staff). Rodrigo our ship videographer spent the last five months in Quito. He is Brazilian, originally from Belo Horizonte but has spent months and years in Ecuador.

AT SEA TOWARD BAHIA October 10th

THE BMW AND FORMULA ONE RACER

Dinner that night was with a terrific couple. The gentleman races BMWs and Ferraris all over the world, Formula 1. He has raced with and knew Paul Newman. His wife can do the design for the car engines. They do Le Mans style racing. He has not raced but has walked the famous course in Monte Carlo (I met them on the snorkel boat yesterday). As one might imagine, the years of racing have taken a toll on his hearing; he uses hearing aids, is impaired but is still driving.

WADE DAVIS'S TALK ON ZOMBIES

Wade's talk on African religions, Haiti and zombies! The book is titled "The Serpent and the Rainbow." Five stars! Elevated, cerebral, but easy to follow and relate to. He has absolute respect for other religions, "They are also reaching their gods," thus the earlier comment on my fear of Xangô. In Haiti there was a case of a proven "zombie," a man back to life after dying. It involved voodoo, secret societies and using a poison from bones of the deceased that causes death symptoms, but the person really does not die. Wade joined the secret society and has wild tales. Buy the book! He mentioned that every time Hollywood wants to do a zombie movie, they give him a call, and he's a bit tired of it.

JACOB EDGARD'S SECOND TALK ON BRAZILIAN MUSIC

Jacob Edgar did a fine talk on Brazilian music. Another "Rookie" mistake by Curran: I took photos of his images on one of the screens in the lounge and was told by someone on staff that this is a definite "no, no." It makes sense because it is private research and material.   In my naïve defense, I was just following the lead of guests I saw doing the same. Jacob is a generous soul and later graciously gave me a Power Point disk of all the presentations. One part is on the origin of "Samba" and takes you through all its stages and then Carnival. A second is on the Bossa Nova and almost all the major Brazilian singers since, including my favorite Chico Buarque de Holanda. This was probably as close as I would ever get to seeing most of the famous musicians and hearing the favorite music I had witnessed over the years in Brazil.

STRESS AGAIN

I am on the internet in the staff office trying to find out more about Oscar Niemeyer, Brazil's most famous architect. Rodrigo the Ship Videographer swears the house of the Rio party is not Niemeyer's, but maybe he designed part of it. He's adamant about this and insists I ferret out the truth for the recap talk. Due to this when I tried to nap after lunch it was impossible; the mind was a 'whirring. Later: Rodrigo was right, the party was not the famous Niemeyer house, but he may have designed a bit of it. The famous one he did design in Rio which you can Google is called "A Casa das Canoas."

ARRIVAL IN SALVADOR AND EVENING ON SHORE EXCURSIONS
October 11th

I was incredibly excited for this return to one of my favorite places and long-time research areas in Brazil, so I think other than the crew I was up the earliest to take in our arrival just after dawn, this my first time by sea. And on the Explorer to boot! I probably had been in Salvador on twenty-five different occasions from the 1960s to 2005, almost all related to research which resulted in three books on Bahian cultural figures: the novelist Jorge Amado, the "cordel" "Boca do Inferno Popular" ["popular hell's mouth"] Cuíca de Santo Amaro, and the "Cordel" poet, publisher, journalist, showman Rodolfo Coelho Cavalcante who claimed 1,700 story-poems of "cordel" during his forty year career, the most prolific of any "cordel" poet-publisher!

SALVADOR DA BAHIA, ITS HISTORY AND IMPORTANCE

Salvador da Bahia, as it is known by the Brazilians, is the 4th largest city in Brazil after Rio, São Paulo and Brasília, a major economic hub of Brazil's Northeast and its most famous tourist site after Rio with its beaches and carnival. Bahia has all the latter and in fact boasts that its carnival is the largest in Brazil, but with an African flavor. This author can attest to its Barra Beach, rated the 3rd best in the world by a European magazine!

The city was founded in 1549, became one of the richest "captaincies" during the colonial period and then capital of all Brazil for almost 200 years until the capital was transferred to Rio in the 19th century. It vies with Rio for its natural attractions and history. It has dozens of miles of pristine white-sand beaches along the Atlantic Coast and one of the most picturesque old city centers of all Brazil (its two-tiered upper and lower cities connected by the famous Lacerda Elevator). There is an entirely separate modern city of skyscrapers and businesses to its north today.

The old city center has the original government buildings from the 16th century, the main plaza, the old Cathedral Plaza with the original Jesuit Church, the most beautiful baroque church in all Brazil, the "São Francisco" church, and the famous "Pelourinho" or Slave Block plaza nearby. Bahia was the center of Brazil's slave trade for 400 years, based on sugar cane originally and tobacco of later days. The lower city with its customs' buildings, port and colorful "Mercado Modelo" are just some of the highlights.

Culturally it is still the center of Afro-Brazilian culture in Brazil, its famous carnival, its folk ballet, its many religious rituals of "Candomblé" and its folk dance-defense art of "Capoeira" and more. Literary figures from the 16th century to now abound, particularly its most famous writer Jorge Amado. And one of Brazil's best known religious shrines combining Catholic and African religions, the Church of Bonfim, is just another attraction.

Arriving to Salvador da Bahia, the Sea Wall, 2013

There was terrific change and growth and new buildings since my last time in 2005. A Personal Aside: I just found out via an email from Josias of "Cuíca de Santo Amaro" movie fame (I did two books on Cuíca, a major poet of Brazil's "cordel" in Salvador) that he talked to my guides and friends in Salvador, Edilene Matos and Carlos Cunha before the filming, but during the filming Carlos refused to be interviewed on film and was in a state of depression. He died shortly thereafter.

FIRST EVENING IN SALVADOR – ILHÉ AHÉ

We were transported by Ilyé Ayé mini-buses (vans) to the Ilyé Ayé Center in Liberdade (I remembered the "cordel" poet Rodolfo Coelho Cavalcante lived in Liberdade and I had interviewed him at his modest house in 1981). Ilhé Ayé is one of the important, if not the most important, of Salvador's version of the Samba Schools of Rio de Janeiro. There were horribly loud drums, nice costumes, and the guests danced later. I talked to the local leader on the way out in the rain.

Wade and I had a chance to talk on the bus on the way home; he wants to know about ASU! He was highly complementary of me, my knowledge and love of Brazil and praised my enthusiasm. Coming from this master of world culture, yours truly was truly grateful.

Ilhé Ayé Greeters

Director of Ilhé Ayé and Curran - A fortuitous conversation

SECOND DAY, SALVADOR, CITY TOURS October 12th

A.M. BAHIA UPPER CITY TOUR

It would be a huge day (I had slept just so-so; this would build to exhaustion). It was getting scary, up at 6:30, off the ship at 8:15. We were all greeted at the port arrival building by the iconic "Bahianas" – ladies dressed in "candomblé" finery with the good-luck bracelets they give the tourists.

Bahiana and Good Luck Bracelets, Salvador

THE FAIR OF SÃO JOAQUIM

Then it was Bus 2 to the market – fair of "Feira de São Joaquim," a very pleasant surprise. I think it was a remarkable success, a surprise to most of the guests who probably were unaware of all that the market showed us of Bahia and its culture. Among other things there were "Candomblé" supplies (for Bahia's major Afro-Brazilian religious rites), all manner of local foods, birds – it was a slice of the real life of a substantial portion of the people of Bahia. This is the fair-market in the lower city that replaced the fair of "Água dos Meninos" of my years in Salvador in the 1960s (and in Jorge Amado's novels). It is primarily for Bahians of the city of lesser income but also for shoppers from all around the "Bay of All Saints."

São Joaquim Market and Chiles, Salvador

This is just a small part of the accoutrements of "Candomblé" statuary used in the rituals. One sees the "Caboclo" or Indian images to the left, Iemanjá the Goddess of the Sea (corresponding to the Catholic Virgin Mary) in the center and St. George on his white steed to the right.

Bahian Ladies Shelling peas, São Joaquim Market

Puppies for Sale, São Joaquim Market

The Bahian lass was more than pleased to have her photo taken for Explorer Staff and Guests.

Bahian Young Lady, São Joaquim Market

.

BUS CAPTAIN FOR THE FIRST TIME IN BRAZIL – ROOKIE MISTAKES

This was my first time as bus captain in Brazil. I forgot the radio, so I had to go back on board to get it. Nervous about the bus count. I liked the Brazilian guide Simone who had great English and we talked a lot in Portuguese.

The excursion would go to the upper city of 16th and 17th century Salvador, the Plaza Tomé de Souza with its statue of the city's founder, the Cathedral – the old Jesuit church before their expulsion from Brazil and all South America in 1767, to the São Francisco church of course of the Franciscans and its "azulejos" in the patio and its great Baroque interior (Ai, ai, ai! Then my camera battery ran out; I had not learned to take spares). The long walk ended at "Pelourinho" [Pillory] Plaza, the old slave block and Brazil's most notorious plaza and the locale today of the "Fundação Casa de Jorge Amado," a place of research, "worship" and publishing success for me, including a friendship with Jorge who wrote the preface to one of my books. In a rush I left a message for Myriam Fraga its director. We all walked down the cobblestones of the "Baixa dos Sapateiros" to the bus; slow traffic to the ship. Photos of the excursion follow.

The Iconic Lacerda Elevator

Iconic Scene – the Lacerda Elevator, Lower City and the Bay, Salvador

Later at the same place Mark was "cornered" by an insistent "Bahiana" who wanted a tip for the photo. In the old days these ladies cooked and sold regional spicy Bahian food on the streets; today they dress up for tourists and the tips, all sponsored by the municipality. I'm sorry and apologize for an ancient corny joke (Irish I think) brought on by all this: "Don't go into the Roundhouse Nellie, they're liable to corner you there."

BAHIAN FOOD AND "BAHIANAS" ON THE STREETS

You can still find the street food – "acarajé, abaré, xinxim de galinha, moqueca de peixe."

Bahiana and Typical Food Stand

"CAPOEIRA" ON THE STREETS

"Capoeira" on the Streets, Salvador

THE "PRAÇA DA SÉ" AND THE OLD JESUIT CHURCH

In the Cathedral Plaza or "Praça da Sé" one sees the original church of the Jesuits from the 16th century. The order was vanquished from all South America in 1767; the church is now the Cathedral in the "Praça da Sé" but the Jesuit father remains watching over it all.

The Old Jesuit Church, Salvador

THE SÃO FRANCISCO CHURCH

The following scenes are of Brazil's most famous church, "São Francisco" with its famous blue-tiled interior patio and its baroque interior. A Franciscan friar told me on a recent trip that the loud drums of the local Bahian "samba schools" like Oludum really give him and the other few priests a headache, especially at night. He lamented the significant drop in vocations to the Order and admitted that the key role of the church is today's tourism.

Patio of the Church of São Francisco

Curran and Portuguese Blue Tiles, São Francisco Church

The Baroque Interior of the São Francisco Church

In this author's mind there is another image of the same interior in the film based on the novel of Jorge Amado, "Dona Flor and Her Two Husbands," when the hero-vagabond Vadinho hits up the parish priest for a loan while admiring the "lascivious" angels in the church!

The Franciscan Friar's main complaint was the noise from the Oludum Drums, but not from this lovely young lady. Famous Bahian singer-composer Dorival Caymmi composed a samba of the times: "O Que É Que A Baiana Tem."

Singer-Composer Dorival Caymmi's Idea of "What Is It That The Bahian Girls Have?"

BRAZILIAN SPIRITUALIST RELIGION – CHICO XAVIER THE "SEER"

In that same busy plaza in front of the São Francisco I ran into, by accident, an important part of Brazilian Culture – a shop dedicated to Brazilian Kardec Spiritualism and its most important "Vidente" or "Seer" Chico Xavier (1910 to 2002). There was no time to alert guests who were on "free time" and scattered in the area shopping or sightseeing, and my time in the shop was perhaps a total of three minutes when I snapped the photo, rushing on the way to the Pelourinho Plaza. It is important to fill in the gaps here, even if just for another minute. Chico from Minas Gerais (as is his cohort Spiritualist healer Arigó) was a Kardec Spiritualist, but one of a kind, he was a "médium" (one who could communicate with spirits) who "saw" writings of the spirits and "wrote" no less than 450 books and thousands of letters using a process called "psychography." He is credited with 50 million books sold. It is of interest that he called his spiritual guide Emmanuel who lived in ancient Rome as Publius Lentulus, was later reincarnated as a priest in Spain and then a professor at the Sorbonne! Chico Xavier channeled diverse spirits and claimed he could write nothing unless they communicated and cooperated. This is just one more aspect of religion in Brazil, not a small one.

PELOURINHO PLAZA AND THE JORGE AMADO FOUNDATION

There was a rush to arrive in the Pelourinho Plaza down the hill from the São Francisco Church and to pop into the Jorge Amado Foundation Building; lamentably it was not on the tour itinerary but could have been due to Amado's importance and personally to Curran for one his books published by the Foundation with a preface by the same Jorge Amado. I popped in, left a message for the director, Mryiam Fraga, and rushed to join the guests carefully making their way down the cobblestones of the plaza to the bus parked below.

P.M. EXCURSION. SALVADOR

After lunch on the ship in the p.m. there was a long bus ride through traffic to the "Dica de Tororó" with "candomblé" statues in the lake and the new soccer stadium for the Copa de 2014 to its side. It was a long, long bus ride. Our guide in the p.m. is Gabriela, 20 years in Bahia but from Argentina. It was tough to understand her English; she picked up information from me for future guiding trips! Some people talked how I added to the bus rides; I did well with the Portuguese and the information, but not so well on the logistics – the radio, the bus count, etc.

"Candomblé" Statues in Tororó Lake and the World Cup Soccer Stadium

Igreja do Bonfim - Salvador

Slogging through the incredible Bahian traffic, two final stops made my day and I hope that of the guests: the first to one of the great pilgrimage sites of all Brazil – the Church of "Bonfim" ["The Good End"] and then an all too short visit (due to traffic delays) to the colorful and iconic inside market of Salvador "The Model Market" ["O Mercado Modelo"] in the lower city. I add that this market was central to my research over decades in Salvador, played a huge role in Jorge Amado's novels including characters at the market, and was the scene of all the major "cordel" writers from the 1940s to the 1980s, two of whom receiving the academic attention of yours truly and three books.

IGREJA DO BONFIM – SALVADOR

This is yet another of Bahia's famous churches but for distinct reasons. Built in the 1770s it housed the image of the crucified Jesus (from Setubal in Portugal) and over the years became known for its miracles attributed to Jesus, thus one of its main features is the "miracle room" where plastic body parts – heads, hands, legs and such – hang from the ceiling, "memories" or "ex-votos" acknowledging miraculous cures (they were of plaster of paris in my visit in 1966). A second and no less important reason for the church's fame is its syncretism of Catholic and Afro-Brazilian religions. On the feast day in January dozens of the ladies of the "candomblé" rite process for the eight kilometers from Salvador's lower city and its first church of "Conceição da Praia," the ladies in all their finery. Once arriving at Bonfim on the Itapagipe Peninsula they proceed to wash the outside steps of the church and lay flowers in homage singing praises in Yoruba (or Nagô) the African slave language associated with "candomblé" in honor of Oxalá or Jesus. They then join the Catholic rituals inside the church. Bonfim is one of a half dozen major pilgrimage sites in all Brazil and the "festa" attracts hundreds of thousands throughout the year.

The visit to Bonfim with LEX was my first since 1966, and along with staff duties I indeed did my own pilgrimage, including an impulsive moment which I kissed the cross of Jesus, the patron saint, at an exposition of the Blessed Sacrament with Christ on the Crucifix (but with no time to formulate a proper prayer request). For our guests, first-timers to Brazil, this was a magnificent lesson in Brazilian culture and folk-popular religions. The "miracle room" or "promises room" with today's plastic arms, legs, hands, heads of humans – the "Ex-votos" – was a revelation to all. As usual, the unexpected came up: an "emergency" trip to the gift shop where there was a small bathroom for one of our guests and a lot of hurried up Portuguese! But it had its reward: she was grateful, and I saw all the stuff they sell to people who come. Bonfim is as major place, glad I was there again. Last time was November 1966!

The "Miracle Room" at the Church of Bonfim, Salvador

Good Jesus in the Gift Shop

And finally, the Afro-Brazilian "Candomblé" Images for sale – in this case the "Pretos Velhos" or "Old Africans" Saints and a bloody St. Sebastian.

The "Old Blacks" and a Bloody St. Sebastian

A Happy LEX Staffer outside the "Igreja do Bonfim"

THE MERCADO MODELO

The "Mercado Modelo" was our last stop. The visit was shortened due to traffic between the peninsula where Bonfim is located and the lower city where the Market stands. LEX people did not know I convinced the bus driver to take a direct route to the market, abandoning a side drive past some far lesser sights thus at least giving us about twenty minutes at the market. Guests were amazed and thrilled and did lament the too short visit. I hope this is remedied in the future – a great place for shopping and Bahian food with a view of the bay.

The Market is the center of folk and tourist life in Salvador's lower city and it has been that way for a hundred years. Not only does it sell all kinds of tourist gadgets ("bugigangas") but some quality clothing based on the Afro-Brazilian rites and on the top floor is an excellent store of semi-precious stones, some of the best in Brazil (the interior of Bahia state has the mines). It also has a beautiful restaurant with the best of Bahian food and a magnificent view of the ships and the bay. And finally, it was the scene of "cordel" poets and their performance of singing and declaiming their verse for decades (as mentioned, Salvador merited three books!) Missing was the truly folkloric scene of the 1960s – the huge fish market, the dense traffic of Bahian small fishing and sail boats, and the market activity, all documented in one of my books.

I did have about two minutes to rush out and meet the "poet-singer" ["cantador"] who was ensconced in Rodolfo Coelho Cavalcante's old poetry stand. And there was a very short conversation with the "new" owners who bought from Caméu de Oxossi of Jorge Amado days.

EVENING. BALÉ FOLCLÓRICO DA BAHIA

Our final stop in this jam packed two days in Salvador was a performance of the Folkloric Ballet of Bahia. That night we all were transported by bus to the "Baixa dos Sapateiros" and its dark streets, the only place for the bus to park. There were many stairs and steps and finally an elevator, walking and weaving through buildings to the theater-restaurant. In that darkness I had "bad vibes" as we walked through the area. However, the restaurant provided us with the best "caipirinhas" of the entire trip.

I intentionally leave out some rough moments on the trip and am emphasizing the positive, but it is both true and just to mention that all was not perfect. Guests on the excursion to Salvador lamented they had had no chance for "real Bahian" food (famous in all Brazil). The Mercado Modelo Market restaurant would have been a remedy. Traffic foiled that! However, the show of amazing music, dancing and Bahian folklore to follow was second to none!

There was a hilarious street scene on the way – Bahian men laughing and joking at a sidewalk domino game.

THE SHOW. BALÉ FOLCLÓRICO DA BAHIA

There was "candomblé, puxa rede, Iemanjá, maculelê, e capoeira" [loosely translated as dances related to the Afro rite of "candomblé," fishermen hauling in their nets, a homage to the goddess of the sea Iemanjá (African saint corresponding to the Blessed Virgin Mary), a stick dance derived from the cut sugar cane in the fields, and finally a performance of "capoeira"]. All was highly stylized but good with correct steps and nuances of the "orixás" or African saints (they did in-depth research in putting this show together). I understand this troupe travels the world. There was some stress in taking the pictures; they were officially "not allowed," but along with many other guests, I took a few with the small camera. Glad I did.

Iemanjá, Goddess of the Sea and the Fishermen Who Worship Her

"Capoeira" at Its Best

We arrived home to the ship and I surmise most of us exhausted from the intense two days stay in Bahia (would not have had it any other way). Steak dinner that night with guests. The Explorer leaves at 10 p.m. from Salvador and it is seven hours to Ilhéus in southern Bahia State with a full day program tomorrow. I wrote, "Priscilla should be on the ship." She is our in-house expert on Rio with her phenomenal best-seller "How To Be a Carioca."

AT SEA TO ILHEUS AND ARRIVAL IN ILHEUS   October 12th, Columbus Day

I ate breakfast with the fellow who designed the thrusters for the Apollo Space Program. He liked our talk of Captain Video, an early black and white tv "space show" of the 1950s, and Werhner von Braun's lectures on the plan to go to the moon on Disney's "Wide World of Color." He quoted Von Braun: "I aimed for the stars, but I hit London." We talked of "The Right Stuff" and Apollo 13 suspense.

This was another instance when I was able to converse with guests; many of them were close to my generation and we shared moments and memories of life. This was a big plus in the total experience.

ILHÉUS

Ilhéus is a large city in southern Bahia State noted for its rich agriculture of tobacco, sugar cane but especially the cacao plantations (Bahia will produce along with Rio Grande do Sul in southern Brazil the best chocolate in all Brazil). And cigar lovers hanker for those stogies. It is a relatively recent phenomenon in the Brazilian economic story, its heyday being the early 20th century when there were land wars and many deaths in the battles for control of the rich soil. There was a wild and wooly "frontier" atmosphere with gun toting bad guys and bodyguards and mercenary fighters for the "Colonels" or rich landowners vying for control and dough. Jorge Amado, Brazil's most famous writer, was born and raised on one of the cacao plantations and wrote early novels of the area's history and strife, the first in stark realism with a Marxist flavor, but later (after Amado learned of Stalin's Gulag and reneged on his Marxist affiliation) delightful, humorous, colorful and entertaining novels of the area, "Gabriela Clove and Cinnamon" being the most famous. LEX will visit the family mansion in Ilhéus and later the famous brothel now nightclub and the Vesúvio Bar where the main characters of Nacib and Gabriela live out the story.

The visit to a working cacao plantation and the rich natural habitat (the Naturalists had a field day with the birding) was an additional highlight, a terrific addition to the Expedition.

ILHÉUS – THE EXCURSION

We arrived on "Nossa Senhora da Aparecida" saint's day; she is the equivalent in Brazil to France's Lourdes and Portugal's Fatima. The excursion passed by Jorge Amado's father's house, now the Amado museum. It was closed when our group went by, but others who caught it were impressed by the old manual typewriter Jorge used to write all the novels. On this the major religious festival day in Brazil, the church was closed. Hmm. Next door was something more important: I ran quickly into the Vesúvio Bar (the scene of much of Jorge Amado's novel, "Gabriela, Clove and Cinnamon"), took photos, not realizing we would return later in the day. This day merits many photos.

This is a tourist shop with the cute clerk standing by the "kitsch" character of Gabriela. Nacib her lover and some-time husband and bar owner is on the shelf to the right.

Staff Member Curran and Statue of Writer-Hero Jorge Amado

An excited Mark rushed to take this first photo of the famous bar of the novel, the Vesúvio, not realizing LEX would return in the p.m.

Curran in Front of the Vesúvio Bar – Restaurant

A "Kitsch" Jorge Amado, A Thinking Pose

Another thing the guests were "thirsting for" was the chance to buy Brazilian souvenirs. Fortunately, on the way to the bus we stopped at a chocolate shop (one of Bahia's best products) and directed the entire crowd inside. Never was there such a good sales day for the store. One guest bought miniature Bahian chocolates for his entire staff of employees, saying it was perfect! One of the finer local delicacies in Brazil is the local liqueur ["licor"] made from an unending variety of fruits, but also of chocolate. Free samples were provided, and many bottles of that good stuff were jammed into homeward luggage (if not imbibed in guest rooms).

The Cacao Plantation

The bus took us to the cacao plantation, 40 kilometers outside Ilhéus and it was a very pleasant surprise. There is once again the already mentioned Jorge Amado connection. He grew up on his parents' cacao plantation near Ilhéus and was witness to or heard from relatives of the famous local battles for land and riches. There are several books: the original "Cacau," "Terras do Sem Fim" but the modern delight "Gabriela, Clove and Cinnamon" tells the story in spectacular fashion in the era of the 1920s.

There was a small glitch when I missed my assigned walking tour, but for a good reason. It turns out someone must "bring up the rear" and keep track of those guests perhaps with walking aids or a recent hip or knee replacement, such was my duty of helping one of the elderly guests back to the bus. I managed after getting her safely to her seat to do a hike alone: saw blue Morpho butterflies, armadillo holes, cutter ants, the river and birds. (I believe there was some criticism for my not staying with the group but taking care of the guest prevented this; by the time I got her to the bus, the tour had gone on far ahead. In fact, I walked into the forest searching for them and did not see them, so it was not my fault). For me, this place had the potential for the best yet for Brazilian nature.

Lunch was served to a thirsty, hot and famished crowd: rice, chicken, beef, beans, flan, cafezinho, real Brazilian food! And icy beer, very welcomed by all the guests. Later there was time to walk through the "fazenda" house, super elegant and reflecting the wealth of the cacao plantation owners.

River running through Cacao Plantation

David Wright and Cacau Trees on the Plantation

Old Cacao Plantation "Big House" and Grounds

Back in town we drove to a small "folk art" market. They sold Bahian Carnival "accouterments" including the "kitsch" men's and women's sex organs! Such items were the props for Vadinho and gang during carnival in Bahia in the movie "Dona Flor." This was indeed a surprise to me and something, modesty or whatever, prevented me from pointing them out to the guests. And in a market stall down the way there on sale were some story-poems of "cordel!"

"Jogo de Búzios," Tarot and "Candomblé" Dress, Gift Shop, Ilhéus

THE VESÚVIO BAR OF "GABRIELA CLOVE AND CINNAMON"

We returned to the Vesúvio Bar, a highlight for me. This was the main scene, made fiction, in Jorge Amado's "Gabriela Clove and Cinnamon." There were cold beers with naturalists and photographers Bud Lenhausen, Tom Richey, and Doug Cothrane, and we saw the amazing arrival of the parakeet flight in the plaza at 5 p.m.

I got to talk to one of my favorite guests, he from Brooklyn and the Bronx; he grew up amidst all the folderol of life on 42 St. in New York! For the Kansas farm boy this was a spicy story.

Then there was a chance for a reunion with the kitsch Jorge Amado.

The Two Thinkers – Jorge Amado and Curran, Vesúvio Bar

HOME TO EXPLORER AND RECAP: DOUG GUALTIERI ON CACAO

WADE AND GAIL DAVIS, DINNER

Dinner: Wade, Gail. She is a fan and friend of Christopher Parkening the fine guitarist whose master classes I attended at Arizona State's fine graduate school of music. Wade seemed "all ears" for my work; pity we could not have known each other years back. He had one suggestion for Lindblad (and he had the experience and knowledge to argue his case): he believes Lindblad needs to challenge the guests and awaken them to things. I don't know if the conversation was just "talk," but he made me feel great and it validated my work. After Wade leaves this trip he goes on an air tour around the world as trip lecturer, then to the U. of British Colombia, as visiting full professor of Cultural Anthropology and Botany, teaching two classes, etc. (I would get a Xmas email a couple of years later explaining his classes in cultural anthropology with 350 students!)

Once again, on the trip, I had great rapport with shore guides who were amazed at my Portuguese, wanted to know of my work; I gave tips to guides in Salvador and Rio.

Tired, I will give the Amado talk at sea tomorrow. We may see whales in the Abrolhos waters.

Chat with Rich Cahill, Panama, naturalist; his wife runs their Panama Resort when he's on ship. He is totally bilingual Spanish-English. He promised the famous "rainbow" bass if I joined him for a trip with Keah.

"JEN, HOW AM I DOING?"

I had a chance to talk to Jen: "How am I doing?" All okay from her end. She asked if I wanted to go on next year's trip? Do I want to go next year? I gave a tentative yes but will decide after this trip. My view: my talks were excellent and went well, good rapport with guests, bus count and radio a negative, a lot to learn. It was a very friendly conversation; she taught me some more use of staff computers. Jen says the second trip is "infinitely easier."

NEXT DAY, CURRAN'S AMADO TALK, AT SEA TO ABROLHOS AND THE WHALES October 13th

A.M. Up at 5:30! I reviewed for the Amado talk, printed a summary page, worked on Rio slides (and saw Rodrigo's video clip of Fernando de Noronha, very professional, funny coming from me with "expertise" on Noronha).

Keah, the Amado talk went super! Can't tell you how many compliments, "personalized, good humor, humble with Jorge." More compliments than first talk.

MARK CURRAN "BAHIA THROUGH THE LENS OF JORGE AMADO"

Placing Jorge Amado:

    a. He was one of the "romancistas do Nordeste" along with Raquel de Queiróz, José Lins do Rego and Graciliano Ramos.

    b. He was a contemporary of Colombia's García Marquez and Peru's Mário Vargas Llosa. They won the Nobel; he did not. He also wrote at the time of Carlos Fuentes, a famous Mexican novelist.

    c. A Best Seller in Brazil; it's bestselling novelist and best known until his death.

    d. He was the heart and soul of Bahia, my "guide" to that part of Brazil.

    e. Famous novels: "Mar Morto," Jubiabá," "Tenda dos Milagres", "Dona Flor e seus Dois Mariodos", " Gabriela Cravo e Canela" (we shall see the scene in Ilhéus).

    II.   Curran in Bahia in 1966

1. To check out "cordel" situation: Cuíca de Santo Amaro, Rodolfo Cavalcante
2. Most important: to get to know this important Brazilian city, old colonial capital, and "city of mystery" of Jorge Amado; "cordel" would have to wait. The goal was to get to really know Bahia. All through the lens of "Bahia de Todos os Santos" by Jorge Amado.
3. The absolute beauty of the setting: the sea and "orla," the long beaches on the east, the upper and lower old city. See "Adventures" from 1966.

Investigating Jorge's Bahia …

By day:

Cidade Alta: Government buildings/ Catedral – Praça da Sé/Terreiro de Jesus/ Igreja de São Francisco/ Old Pelourinho/ Nossa Senhora do Rosário/ Baixa dos Sapateiros/ Funicular/ Igreja de Santa Bárbara/ Praça dos Quinze Mistérios/ and Elevador Lacerda

Cidade Baixa: "saveiro" dock, fish Market, Loide Lines, Bahiana Line, and especially the Mercado Modelo with Cordel poets/Feira de Água dos Meninos/ Igreja do Bonfim - Oxalá

By night:

Capoeira/ some candomblé/ out with friends to clubs/ see "City of Mystery," including Jorge Amado's old "Tabaris" Club

"A Portuguesa" on Avenida 7; dorm near Piedade Plaza; restaurant in the Barra and swimming. The Portuguese Experience

III.   Research on Later Trips

1981: work on "cordel" poet Cuíca de Santo Amaro, his pauper grave at the cemetery, Cuíca's widow, library work

Work on Rodolfo Coelho Cavalcante at Mercado Modelo and interviews in Liberdade

Amado book comes out in 1981 – "Comemoração dos 50 Anos"

1985: Lessa Prize, tourism with Keah.

1990: Cuíca book comes out

Tourism, Friends 1988, 1989, 1990, 2000 and 2005, 2013 Lindblad-National Geo Brazil

Cf. Pierre Verger, photography/ Jorge Amado, novels/ Castro Alves Poetry

THE WHALES - ABROLHOS

After the talk, we were all called to the bridge, whale watching and cameras. There were maybe six whales and we watched for one and one-half hours. Captain Oliver runs the Explorer like a speed boat, basically in circles around the pods and keeping us all informed on the ship p.a. system (At recap tonight one of the features will be by Tom Richie on the whales.) Cows – calves, two pods. Even Captain Oliver marveled!

Curran, Patrik and Captain Oliver on the Bridge

Momma Whale Up Clos

An Important Aside: Food and Meals on Board

The meals were healthy beginning with delicious morning and noon buffets. The evening was fine dining and "special." Tonight before dinner there was sangria and grilled chicken on the back deck. I should comment that the "special food events" on the back deck in the p.m., the regular 4 o-clock tea time, the snacks at recap and then dinner were more than enough to satisfy the most seasoned travelers among the guests.

Recaps Are Great

Recaps continue to be great and perhaps a highlight of the day. I have only done one thus far – an Introduction to Salvador via "capoeira" and "candomblé." This is when the Naturalists shine!

Tonight's featured Rich Cahill on dye and Indians. He is relaxed and funny. His wife runs the tour resort in Panama (as mentioned, he promised "rainbow bass.")

Then Dennis Cornejo – a jewel in the rough! Plants, termites and ants. Funny!

Then Tom Richey – whales!

Wade and Gail Davis, the Classic Guitar

Dinner was swordfish, Brazilian "açai" ice cream. Gail continued her wonderful "education" on Classic Guitar. She spoke of Danube Rosewood, proper technique, and, get ready guitar fans – the care of fingernails. She has two fine guitars and encouraged me to get a prompt appraisal on my own Di Giorgio Rosewood Brazilian guitar from 1966.

If Wade is a 10, I'm a 1 or 2, my good fortune. I'm reading "The River" from the library.

I have to work on the Rio introduction for tomorrow 2:30 p.m. Rodrigo is still placing doubts about Niemeyer house. (See "Why Rio?" and my experience as well.)

THE NEXT DAY, AT SEA, TALKS AND MY EDUCATION CONTINUES
October 14th

"WILDLIFE IN THE SOUTH ATLANTIC," RICHARD WHITE "Wildlife in the South Atlantic," Richard White

Whales, petrels, penguins, etc.

BOSSA NOVA AND JACOB EDGAR

Great talk by Jacob on the "Bossa Nova;" he gave me the down loads.

An Aside: a San Francisco couple, she Asian – American. They want to look up a friend in Rio, a French restaurant owner in Rio. How to get a taxi.

RECAP: "INTRODUCTION TO RIO DE JANEIRO," MARK CURRAN

Lots of preparation for Rio intro. Dennis Cornejo wires me up. Went great. Very complimentary from Jen, David, Wade and David Cothrane. Cocktail hour and guests. Staff really supports each other, camaraderie.

I got to talk a bit to Dennis Cornejo (U of A in Tucson), does undersea diving, snorkeling for guests, and plant life. Had tale/ photo of Pete Poulson with baby alligator in his mouth. They all have done such things for years. Wade Davis since 1981 with Lindblad, Tom Ritchie and Jen Martin, too, Tom's daughter Laurel Ritchie is on staff.

My Notes on "Introduction to Rio" (only a very small part of which were included in the talk, but as research on my part – an "extra" for readers of this book).

2014. INTRODUCTION TO RIO. Mark Curran

Images.

1. Downtown, Santos Dumont Airport
2. Glória, Passeio Público, Aterro Park on a Sunday
3. Airport, Glória, Flamengo, Botafogo, "Yate" Club, Sugar Loaf, Copa, Fort, Ipanema-Leblon, Dois Irmãos, São Conrado
4. Cristo Redentor – Corcovado

5. Cristo and a little joke
6. Botafogo Bay and Sugar Loaf from Corcovado, favela on hill to left
7. Cable car to Sugar Loaf taken from Corcovado (sugar loaf from plantations; one mtn. outside of Phoenix, same name, same shape).
8. Old Cable Car in 1967: rain, floods, generators out, car stalled in air
   Today: modern, generators
9. Copacabana in 1966
10. Sidewalks of Rio: Mosaic from Robert Burle Marx, Landscape artist for Brasilia (Curran went to the beach in 1973 instead of tour of his place. Walk on black or white and "do the samba.)"
11. Ipanema on a nice day: "frescobol," beach etiquette. Twenty minutes to settle into your group and Posto.
12. Ipanema at dusk. Girl from Ipanema now a grandmother.
13. New Year's Eve. Copacabana
14. Umbanda, New Year's Eve
15. Getting ready for Carnival, 1967
16. Salgueiro Samba School Dancer ["Passista"] my photo and cover of "Manchete"
17. Old Senate Rio
18. Confeitaria Colombo
19. "Bonde," street car to Santa Teresa, "Orféu Negro"
20. Maracanã Football Stadium. 1950, lose to Uruguay. Win in 1958.
21. Santos Dumont Airport from Urca (shuttle flights between São Paulo and Rio)
22. Oscar Niemeyer as young man, Died at 104 yrs. In 2004.
23. Niemeyer's Works in Pampulha, Minas Gerais. Church of São Francisco de Assis
24. Edifício Copan, São Paulo
25. Congresso em Brasília
26. Itamarati or Aeronáutica, modern sculptures, Brasília
27. Catedral de Brasilia
28. Neimeyer sketches

Notes on History of Rio de Janeiro -More than you need to know!

1. The French enter the Bay of Guanabara in 1555. The Portuguese fight to throw them out from 1565 to 1567. During the battle Portuguese General Mem de Sá (of Salvador fame) was killed.
2. The "Carioca" Personality: the "malandro" made famous in the song by Noel Rosa, "Pelo Telefone." The white linen suit (used by "Comissão de Frente" of a Samba School and the introduction to Chico Buarque de Holanda's "Ópera do Malandro").
3. Bahia was still the "seat" of Brazil's "captanias" and became Brazil's first capital in 1660.

4. In the 18th century (1700s) gold was discovered in Minas Gerais. There was European migration to Brazil and Rio de Janeiro grows, as a port.

5. In 1763 the national capital was moved to Rio. There was an economic crisis when the flow of gold diminished and a drop as well in sugar cane production. But coffee came to Brazil and the Portuguese Royal Family in 1808. Rio grew and prospered.

6. In 1815 Brazil is declared a "kingdom"; Dom Pedro I and II would rule through most of the 19th century.

7. The 19th century was the time of real growth in Rio: the National Theater, the National Library, the Rio Botanical Garden, the Emperors' Palms.

8. There was an increase in coffee plantations in Rio de Janeiro State and the economy grew. The most iconic street in old downtown Rio the "Rua do Ouvidor" was established; the system of transportation developed (the trains by the British), and the Ferry to Niteroi.

9. In 1889 with Independence Rio was declared Capital of the Republic.

10. In 1906 they developed its showcase avenue, "Avenida Rio Branco".

11. In the mid-20th century there were migrants to Rio from the dry Northeast, highways built, skyscrapers in Rio, residential districts, financial centers. Rio was second in economics only to São Paulo.

12. Dates of various monuments in Rio:

1565. City is founded: São Sebastião do Rio de Janeiro its official name

1743. The "Paço Imperial" or Imperial Palace was built in the Old Praça 15 area facing the bay

1750. The Carioca Aqueduto

1783. The "Passeio Público" near Glória.

1808. Rio was now capital of the Kingdom with the Portuguese Dynasty – the Braganças.

1811. Candelaria church was built

1822. Rio became the capital of an Independent Brazil

1854. Catete Palace was built in Flamengo (the place of suicide of President Getúlio Vargas in 1954); It would be the national palace until Brasília opened in 1960.

1858. "Central do Brasil" Train Station opened

It was the British who brought the white linen suit to Brazil; it became national dress.

1877. The Trolley Car "O Bonde" to Santa Teresa in service

1884. The Corcovado railroad was started, but there was no Christ figure yet.

1904. Avenida Rio Branco was finished.

1909. The Teatro Municipal was finished.

1922 The Hotel Glória was completed.

1923. The Copacabana Palace was completed as well as Parque Guinle.

1926. The Hippodrome "Hipódromo" or race track in Laranjeiras was finished.

1931. The Cristo Redentor Statue was completed.

1936. Santos Dumont Airport was completed.

1940. The PUC was completed, Pontifical Catholic University

The 1940s: casino gambling was legal; some say 1947 the best year to live in Rio

1950. Maracanã Soccer Stadium is opened but with a surprise loss to Uruguay. Brasil would only win the cup in 1958 with Pelé and Garrincha.

1960. The national capital is moved to Brasília.

I lament: the Senate Building on Avenida Rio Branco, an architectural jewel, is torn down. Cinelândia in its place.

1961. Tijuca Forest is developed for tourism. Also "Edificio Avenida Central" then Rio's biggest skyscraper.

1965. Flamengo Aterro Park is built.

1972. The Petrobras Building is built; its home base.

1976. The Meridien Hotel in Copacabana is built.

1977. Rio Centro Shopping is built; also the Rio Othon Hotel.

1979. The Metrô is started.

1979. The UFRJ is begun: Universidade Federal do Rio de Janeiro

1981. Barra Shopping

1993. The Candelaria Massacre

Filipino Night - Philippine night, staff dressed in formal, beautiful native finery. Women beautiful in costumes. I'm getting to know the guests a bit, but it is a challenge with well over one hundred on board. And staff bit by bit. All the latter are off to other ships after this one to all over the planet. No one goes home like me to retired life.

THE NEXT DAY DAWN ARRIVAL IN RIO AND THE BAHIA DE GUANABARA - CITY TOURS October 15th

See the history and highlights of Rio in my previous notes from the "Introduction to Rio" talk.

Dawn Arrival in Rio, Ferry Boats to Niterói across the Bay from Rio, Sugar Loaf

A.M. I AM ONCE AGAIN BUS CAPTAIN ON N. 3 TO CORCOVADO

We all were on the jammed tourist cog train to the top, then walked the seemingly never-ending steps to the base of the Christ Statue. Prior to loading on the cog train all the LEX people with their big cameras got a rare sight – a Toucan nest with two birds at the most unlikely spot on the trip – the patio of the Cog Train Station. (I would look again in 2014 and 2016, no such luck.) I was starved for some reason and purchased another rare thing, a Brazilian style hot dog (with hot peas and corn in addition to the onion, mustard and huge hot dog itself). I took a nostalgic photo of Wade and Gail Davis on top, and of Tyrone Turner in the crowds (he returned the favor of me, disheveled by my pack and camera). It was hazy; my best pictures of Corcovado will come from the later trip on a beautiful day in 2016.

City photos were basically "nostalgia" for me: the 19th century mansion in Copacabana, the Hotel Novo Mundo, Rio Branco Avenue and the Benedictine Monastery. Each year (2013, 2014, 2016) was very different and different scenes are important for each diary. Beach weather and Corcovado and Sugar Loaf weather in 2013 were lousy, but the Cathedral and Benedictine Monastery were great and not repeated. Home for "hot" lunch.

The Brazilian Hot Dog at the Cog Train Station, Corcovado

The Christ Statue Above and the Old Cog Train Car

Magnificent Toucan at the Cog Train Station

Sugar Loaf, Botafogo, Ipanema and Leblon from Corcovado

Curran and the Christ Figure

Wade and Gail Davis, Corcovado

Tyrone Turner and the Crowds at Corcovado

125th ANNIVERSARY OF NATIONAL GEOGRAPHIC SOCIETY AND MAGAZINE – THE CELEBRATION IN RIO DE JANEIRO

This was the culmination of the entire LEX trip down the east side of South America – "Epic South America." It was a wonderful party and deserves a commentary. The bus ride through moderate Rio traffic took from one to one and one-half hours through the north zone to upper Laranjeiras. The guest house contracted by LEX-NGO for the celebration was surrounded by trees that you walk by on a long stairway to the house: then one sees the beautiful glass building and the gardens. An aside: as per Rodrigo Moterani's preoccupation, and he was right, this was not the "Casa das Canoas" by Brazil's most famous architect Oscar Niemeyer, but I did read that the property is owned by the Niemeyer family. This is the Rio I never got to see before! We started with good, tasty "caipirinhas" out on the lawn; I escaped inside before it all started to take pictures of flowers and décor. The cooks were busy doing the big "churrasco" [Brazilian barbecue]; tables were set with nice china, silverware, and glass. Back to the lawn to socialize, then inside. There was soft, great Bossa Nova music in the background (as befitted the classy occasion and crowd). After dinner with Jacob Edgar and a guest of American Field Service days, there was the formality: The National Geographic tribute with the photographers highlighted: Cotton, Sisse, Tyrone, David Wright, and David Cothrane.

Then the show started: vignettes of carnival - "samba de roda, porta-estandarte, capoeira," and the "mulatas" in all their silicone glory. Guests danced; one of the "mulatas" tried to drag me out to dance; I refused because I would have missed the pictures. Just a super night. All arranged by Ralph Hammellbacker the main organizer of LEX-NGO trips who flew in from Miami for the big party. A happy moment was meeting Priscilla Ann Goslin at the end of the evening on the patio, she of "How To Be a Carioca" fame who unfortunately had to miss her role as our host in Rio due to illness.

Locale for the 125th National Geographic Party, Rio

Preparing the Churrasco

The Big Moment – the National Geographic Photographers Featured

Naturalist Doug Gualtieri in Party Mode

Naturalist Dennis Cornejo

"Berimbau" Player Accompanies "Capoeira"

"Capoeira" Performance

Flag Bearer, "Porta-Estandarte" for the Samba School Parade

Samba School Dancers – "Passistas de Escola de Samba"

RIO DE JANEIRO, DAY TWO, EXCURSIONS October 16th

It's a sad day for me in one sense: Wade and Gail Davis leave the ship today. Up at 6 a.m. It was rough. No rest for the wicked, quick breakfast, grab bottle water, radio and off to Bus 3. Ricardo was our new guide and we really hit it off. The morning excursion was jammed with goodies: Sugar Loaf Mountain via the cable cars, the Rio "space capsule" Cathedral, the famed Brazilian National Oil Company – Petrobras - building and protest, old 19th Century Empire building with "O Paço Real" [The Royal Palace of the Braganças in the early 1800s] (in the rain), "Rua do Ouvidor." Church of Mercaderes, "Confeitaria Colombo, Mosteiro de São Bento" with orquids in its trees, the walk to port and rain all day.

SUGAR LOAF MOUNTAIN

Known as "Pão de Açúcar" in Portuguese (because of the similarity in shape to the old sugar cane molds for raw, hard sugar in the Northeast), the gneiss - granite rock rises about 1300 feet above its entrance to the Bay of Guanabara in Rio. Truly an iconic site, its cable cars take people from the base of Babilônia Hill (scene of the "favela" of the same name in "Black Orpheus") to Urca Hill, then a second, longer ride to the top of Sugar Loaf. If you get proper weather the views are the best in Rio, but clouds, smog, and fog can and do come. I was on the original cable car in 1967 when storms cut off electricity in Rio de Janeiro and the cars relied on old generators; we were stranded in the breeze for a few minutes (those old cars started in 1912), but new, large, plastic windowed cars allow us 360-degree views in 2013.

There is no better cultural image to show the entrance to the cable cars to the iconic Sugar Loaf mountain than this gorgeous macaw of gold and amethyst semi-precious stones in the entrance lobby. I have not mentioned that Brazil is perhaps a world leader in the mining, cutting and selling of topaz, amethyst, aquamarine and tourmaline stones. As a young student in Rio in 1967 a girl friend's mother who admired such things arranged for me to buy a handful of the cut stones for a pittance, but don't tell my wife Keah how much; she was the primary benefactor!

Topaz-Amethyst Parrot, Sugar Loaf

It was a hazy day in Rio (better days were to come in 2016) so pictures are limited. First, the view of famous Copacabana Beach from the top of Sugar Loaf.

Copacabana from Sugar Loaf

Then came the view looking back to Corcovado and the Christ Statue with yours truly in foreground. You can see the cable cars headed up and down from Urca Hill and Botafogo Bay with its yacht club on this cloudy, hazy day. My main research place in Rio was amidst the tall buildings in the back of the Bay and my first days in Rio were spent as a guest in a luxury apartment on the right in Flamengo.

Corcovado, Cable Car and Curran, Sugar Loaf

Best was this shot of a group of Brazilian tourists from the interior seeing THEIR Brazil!

We saw a beautiful bright red feathered song bird, but the photo did not do it justice. And finally, the ubiquitous marmoset "saguí" monkeys who drive all crazy in the Urca Café, especially cleaning up after the ice cream sodas!

RIO'S METROPOLITICAN CATHEDRAL

After Sugar Loaf we visited Rio's Modern Cathedral in downtown Rio, a conical structure which reminded me of the U.S. space capsule of John Glen fame in the Air and Space Museum on the Mall in Washington, D.C. They claim it was inspired by Mayan Pyramids! It was built from 1964 to 1979 during the military regime and is quite a sight with its conical form and the many rows of stained glass on the inside (four rectilinear - you hope for a sunny day) and ultra-modern statuary inside. It is dedicated to the patron saint of Rio, St. Sebastian, and carries his name. It is almost 100 meters across and a height of almost 75 meters, in other words, huge. There are wooden benches with no kneelers (seating capacity 20,000, standing 5,000), avant-garde statues of saints and Jesus on the Cross as well as an outstanding modern version of St. Francis. Pope John Paul II visited early on. If it is not sunny the immediate impression is of an immense dark, gloomy place, but when that sun comes out it does an about face and is startling in its beauty.

An added note I captured is an iconic part of old Rio, but not today: the old telephone booths prior to today's cell phone world which I estimate 90 per cent of the Cariocas use. Brazilian humor rules: the Brazilians called the booths "the big ear" or "orelhão" and of course the first and most common greeting is "Oi!" ["Hi!".]

Interior of the Cathedral, Stained Glass and Cross

THE PETROBRAS BUILDING AND NATIONAL POLITICAL SCANDAL

Adjacent to the Cathedral is a landmark once symbolizing the grandeur and progress of modern Brazil – the glass and steel ultra-modern Petrobrás building – the home of one of Brazil's largest bureaucracies (in a country famous for its bureaucracy), the national oil company. Brazil's economic fortunes took an upturn in recent decades when large pools of oil were discovered in deep water off shore in the Atlantic; since then a massive drilling effort took place with the huge floating oil rigs one sees from Bahia to Rio Grande do Sul. That's the good news.

The bad news is that it brought in huge amounts of income and the opportunity for Brazil's favorite pastime: political and economic corruption on a scale unimaginable even in Brazil. Private contractors for services and construction overcharged the company for the above, "oiling" the squeaky hinges of Petrobras Executives' Offices and added a steady flow of payoffs to the political parties, including the Workers' Party [PT], President Lula's party. His chosen successor Dilma although not proven directly involved eventually was impeached and replaced by a right-wing president and cronies also wrapped in the scandal. Brazil was outraged, heads fell, the economy tanked, and we on LEX drove by protests on Avenida Rio Branco. The huge anti-corruption campaign of "Lava-Jato" or "Carwash" continues, and only a Brazilian expert can possibly explain it all. (LEX had such a man as a featured speaker on our next trip of 2014, Alberto Pfeifer.) My research on the modest "Literatura de Cordel" even got into the act, the poets writing and publishing dozens of fiercely satiric story-poems on the scandals including the "money in the shorts" incident when a money launderer was caught in one of the international airports with, well, his shorts stuffed with 100-dollar bills). At the time of this writing, Ex-President Lula is in jail and a good many of the people running Brazil are equally mired in corruption.

Petrobras Building, Rio

THE OLD DOWNTOWN RIO

On that rainy day in 2013 we were not blessed by the Brazilian weather gods; there was light to heavy rain a good part of the day. We donned our raincoats and pulled out the umbrellas and did a long walk through the old part of downtown Rio de Janeiro; one must know where one is going and have some knowledge of the 19th century to appreciate it. The walking excursion passed the old Portuguese Royal Palace (the palace created in Rio in 1743 and coming into prominence when Portugal was under control of Napoleon Bonaparte and the Portuguese royal family had fled to Brazil in 1808 and Portugal only was freed when British General Wellington helped patriots in Portugal throw out Napoleon in 1814), but there was no time to go inside. A few other landmarks of that plaza remain but I think it is more important to show shots of what our guests might recognize plus a couple of Brazilian cultural jewels that I pointed out to those stragglers on the tour (the group leader missed such sights or did not want to talk about them.) I was, as usual, bringing up the rear, watching for LEX stragglers with a tendency to wander off the chosen path when curiosities arose. And they did.

This is where Carmen Miranda of musical and cinematic fame originally lived in Rio; Carmen was from Portugal, naturalized with her family in Rio and became that "kitsch" national icon with the fruit on her hat and "pseudo" Bahian dress.

A SURPRISE ENCOUNTER WITH THE NUMBERS' RACKET ["O JOGO DO BICHO"]

This nondescript photo I got on the tour has an importance far beyond its appearance. Our guide was too busy to point out the fellow, but Curran knew. This is a national phenomenon: a "bicheiro" or numbers' racket salesmen of the illegal (but what else, nationally popular) lottery. These guys don't have offices but do their bookkeeping on the streets near their customers. It's a major part of Brazilian folklore, the lottery coming from a ticket procedure at the national zoo in the 19th century in Rio de Janeiro when folks buying tickets to get in received the ticket receipt with an animal image on it – lion, bear, giraffe, ostrich and the like - for a door prize. Like so many things Brazilian, that is, accidental, the ticket scheme was "borrowed" by hoodlums and evolved into today's multi-million dollar national "illegal" lottery. I can't begin to explain it all but can say it has become an important part of Brazilian folklore: people regularly interpret their dreams of animals into hunches for buying that day's lottery ticket. The lottery has a reputation for being the most honest corruption in all Brazil, it you win you get your money! Tickets are hand-written "chits" you take back to your dealer the next day and get your cash! The most common bet is one "real" or about 50 cents U.S.D. So, we at LEX walked right by one of these "businessmen" at work. An aside: it is widely rumored and accurate that the huge national Carnival celebration with the Samba Schools and their parade has been sponsored with huge wads of cash by the "bicheiros" now a crime syndicate in Rio.

Numbers' Racket "Jogo do Bicho" at Work

CANDELARIA CHURCH, ICON AND NATIONAL TRAGEDY

And finally, on our way back to the ship we walked by another iconic church in Rio, "A Candelaria" (with a female impersonator swishing by outside), the church built over the years after 1775, Baroque façade and Neo-Classic interior, known for being inaugurated by King João VI of Portugal while in Brazil fleeing Napoleon. It was also known in modern times in recent years for the "Candelaria Massacre," a planned operation by para-military or off-duty police to "disappear" the many street children who slept at night in the doorways and along the walls of the church. Many of the latter were murdered in cold blood and it became a national scandal. Most recently it was the scene of the major protests in 1984 at the end of the Military Dictatorship calling for direct elections for President of Brazil. The "cordel" story-poems told it all for their public in Rio!

"CONFEITARIA COLOMBO," RIO'S TEA SHOP

What we did not miss, and it truly was a highlight of that short afternoon in Rio was the planned visit to the "Confeitaria Colombo," a cultural and gastronomic highlight of the city. Founded in 1894 with Art Deco and "Belle Époque" architecture and décor it soon became THE gathering spot for socialites, politicians, intellectuals and artists and the aspiring public for afternoon tea, parties and social moments and great food especially the desserts. It was the primary spot in Rio to see and be seen. The huge mirrors from Belgium with the Brazilian rosewood frames, the gorgeous stained-glass ceiling plus the food, great demitasse coffee and desserts made it a thriving place, still the same today with LEX's visit.

Stained Glass Ceiling, Art Deco, "Confeitaria Colombo," Rio

Mirrors in Rosewood Frames, Belgian Glass, Confeitaria Colombo, Rio

THE BENEDICTINE MONASTERY ["O MOSTEIRO BENEDITINO"]

The city tour that morning ended with a truly important, historic and iconic part of the city of Rio de Janeiro – the Benedictine Monastery – begun in 1590 donated from land on Benedictine Hill in downtown Rio to two Benedictine monks from the famous monastery in Bahia. Construction throughout the 17th and 18th centuries resulted in the Baroque masterpiece. Equally famous was the Benedictine school to its side with some of the most famous Brazilians as graduates including Pixinguinha, Noel Rosa and Heitor Villa – Lobos of Brazilian music fame. Curran had a private tour of the monastery in 1967 through connections at my rooming apartment that culminated in lunch in the refectory with the monks and eating in silence with scripture readings. LEX guests were fortunate to have this visit including the beautiful "mangueira" trees outside with the splendid orchids in their branches; anyone familiar with the cities of the world and cultural tourism realizes that at any given moment or year there may be remodeling ["em obras"] and such places being closed; such was the case in the later 2014 trip.

Interior, Benedictine Monastery, Rio

That beautiful, baroque interior contrasted with the style of the Brazilian baroque façade – a plain, undecorated outside wall characteristic of the times.

After the monastery it was back to the ship, exhausted, and eating a quick lunch before the intense afternoon to come. The reader notes that this portion of the book is weighted with cultural anecdote, in part because that was my job on Explorer, but also because the places and moments I describe are indeed icons of Brazil, its cities, culture and peoples, and a major part of "Epic South America."

P.M. "SAMBA CITY" AND PROVIDENCIA "FAVELA"

A Curran "Extra:" Explaining Rio's Carnival

Rio's Carnival is the most famous in the world and LEX guests already knew a lot about it (some from my "Introduction to Rio" recap before arrival). What we saw that afternoon was part of it, the Portela Samba School production shop where the huge carnival floats are prepared for the grand competition, and a visit to one of the "favelas" now called communities that make up the significant percentage of the people in the famous Samba Schools.

There is one night above all others that makes Carnival famous, that is, the "Sapucaí" Carnival, the great night of the parade of the Samba Schools on Presidente Vargas Avenue in the center of Rio. On the long night and next day, the gamut of Rio revelers passes in parade. My own experience was ten days of reveling written about in "Adventures of a 'Gringo' Researcher in the1960s in Brazil." Carnival has changed drastically but is essentially the same as I described based on that experience. I add that even with the brilliance and spectacle of the show in 1966, it was still "pure" as the folklorists would say.

The first to parade were the "Societies" ["Sociedades"], the big carnival floats with allegorical themes; I recall costumes of the bull of "Bumba Meu Boi," of northeastern cowboys, huge bumblebees, and then the Model-T cars (a carryover of the first carnival parades of "calhambeques" or "Model – T's," of upper class Cariocas at the beginning of the 20th century). The floats, all interesting, had a moral and political aside: the beautiful "mulatas" riding on the floats and dancing samba were not topless! The Military Protectors of the Nation and its morality would of course not permit such a thing in 1967.

Then came the "cream," the famous Samba Schools (one always remembers the Samba School of "Black Orpheus"), by far the most impressive part of all Carnival for me. There were literally thousands of participants in each Samba School, each group from one of the poor "favelas" of Rio, mainly black and "mulatto" participants, but with a smattering of white dancers ("wannabes" from TV or the movies or even upper-class Rio), each School with a theme and a theme song memorized and sung by all as they danced down the avenue in front of the spectators and the reviewing stand. The schools were highly organized with a fixed structure (one can perhaps include the entire phenomenon as a part of Brazilian Folklore; this was how it seemed to me). First came the "Comissão de Frente" [the "Board" at it were]. I remember one case when all, perhaps eight or nine men, were jet black and dressed in brilliantly white linen suits with a red carnation in the lapel - "this" was the "classic" clothing worn by the stereotyped Carioca "malandro" [slick rogue], an icon of old Rio.

Then came the "Passistas," the "star" dancers of each school, men and women, followed by a beautiful girl carrying the banner of the school, the "Porta-Estandarte" [A smattering of these figures is what we all saw at the party for the 125th]. These dancers were the best! Then came the "wings" or divisions of the large total group ["as azas"], each with variations on the costumes and representing an aspect of the overall theme, comprising perhaps a thousand dancers. Then came the "bateria," the percussion section, also perhaps totaling hundreds of all manner of drums and percussion instruments. It was this group, all in unison, that maintained the "rhythm" and "beat" of the name "Samba School."

I recall the Salgueiro Samba School with its theme of "freedom," the red and white colors, a sub - theme of Tiradentes, a Brazilian martyr for Independence from Portugal, the abolition of slavery, all in incredibly rich costumes. Then came a traditional part of all the schools - the "Bahian Lady" wing - black ladies of all shapes and sizes, but most "big sized" with the huge skirts reminiscent of the Bahian "candomblé" costumes. There was also the school of Vila Isabel: costumes, dancers, percussion, and then Mangueira, perhaps the most famous school of all in its colors of pink and green! The night was long, and for me tiring; each school took from one to two hours to pass the reviewing stand, and there were many schools, a true Brazilian spectacle! We were standing the entire time, the wooden bleachers vibrating up and down with the flow of the "samba dancing."

The parade would go into the wee hours and then into daylight of the next day. Still awake, we experienced the dawn of that Carnival morning, a long, colorful and romantic time bringing back memories of "Black Orpheus" when Orpheus walked in the wet streets of dawn on Ash Wednesday, carrying his deceased lover Eurídice to the top of the hill opposite Urca and the denouement of the film. Due to a small but good camera, but now without a flash or batteries after six months in Brazil, I took few slides of Carnival, but did get one memorable one that morning along Getúlio Vargas Avenue - the lady was one of the "Passistas" of Salgueiro and appeared on the cover of one of the national magazines' coverage of Carnival that week.

What we now were to see was the huge warehouse, factory and creative nexus of one of the famous Carnival Schools of the 2013 era: that of Portela. I'm in Van 2 with David Cothrane, Ralph Hammellbacker and Jacob Edgar (the latter two talked music the entire time). We all visited the Portela Samba School prep site for next year, including the iron frames and scaffolding to build huge floats, huge Styrofoam figures, a horrible glue smell, costumes, and a very brief meeting with Alexandre, 30 years a 'Carnavalesco' like Joãozinho Trinta from my days; Alexandre has won the big one for Portela. He was the creative genius, combined producer and director of the entire affair.

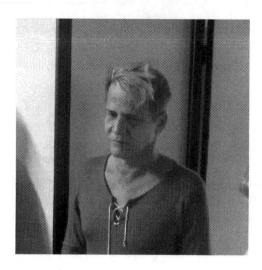

Alexandre, the "Brains" Behind Portela Samba School

The Portela Compound was followed by a long drive up to the very top street in Providência "Favela," now called "comunidade," then there were 80 tall concrete steps to the top and a view of downtown, the port, and the Rio-Niterói Bridge through rain, mist and smog. Many children of the "Providência Percussion Club" and teenagers put on a drum and dance show. The social club served cake and "caipirinhas" for all. These kids are prepping for their roles in the coming Samba parades and represent a small slice of the bigger picture in Rio. The drum "captain" ran the show and I've never seen such efficiency in anything else in Brazil – his whistle commands were right out of the samba school parades. For many guests the performance of the Providência kids and being IN a Rio "favela" was more impressive than Corcovado or Pão de Açúcar. It also was a first time for me, fascinating for the excellent work the "comunidade" is doing for youth activities but also for the impressive view of Rio from their social center – the downtown, the port and bay of Guanabara. We were there in day time, escorted by several police and there was no sign of the dark reality so familiar to Brazilians and foreigners of the crime, poverty and misery to be found in such places. There will be significant changes in 2014 to be detailed later.

A View from "Providencia – Favela – Comunidade"

A Teenager Shows His Fancy, Improvised Samba Steps

The Percussion "Captain"and Future Star of Samba Parades

As staff I was one of the very last to leave the scene in view of the duty of making sure we had no curious stragglers. It turned out to be fortuitous – most guests took the 80 steps back down, but I was told by the armed policeman we were going down the "back way." It turned out to be a walk back down through the interior of the "favela" with views of its classic spider web of electric lines (the "favelas" are famous for their pirating of electricity from the city pool), a boy watching color TV, police on all sides. It was a labyrinth of "favela" homes (these are what are being rented out to tourists for the World Cup and the Olympics; I read pro and con; it is still dangerous up there. I just read of murders in "Rocinha" Favela where I accidentally got lost on a bus ride some years ago).

Pirated Electricity – An Electrician's Nightmare and a "Favela" Dweller's Dream

One of the Dwellings in "Providência

I can't leave out a snapshot of Brazilian folklore I have been writing and lecturing about for years: the clay dolls from Brazil's Northeast ["bonecos de barro"], a truly folkloric phenomenon in the 1960s with Master Vitalino, and the evolution of the same to be sold in the airports, swank shops of Copacabana and Ipanema, and now as I discovered on the return to the ship from Providência, the port of Rio.

Northeastern Folklore in Touristy Rio

We arrived "home" to the ship, I exhausted, a light dinner, and I made a decision to miss the nightclub and samba show at the "Scenarium" in Rio (I would see it in 2014 and 2016). I was scary tired by this time and just did not trust myself to the night of revelry, but the guests and the naturalists had a fun time. I'll show it all in 2014 and 2016. I cleaned up, wrote a long e-mail to Keah, did these travel notes and began organizing for Paraty. To bed 9:30

OCTOBER 17TH ARRIVAL, TOUR AND TERRIFIC LUNCH IN PARATY

Explorer's next stop would be one of the most famous tourist-vacation spots in all Brazil, the beach resort of Paraty on the coast southeast of Rio and on the border with São Paulo State. Established in 1667 by the Portuguese, it was originally inhabited by the Guaianás Indians, but became important as the end of the "Gold Trail," a rough, cobblestoned road linking Paraty port to the gold fields of the interior state to the west Minas Gerais in the 18th century, a 1200-kilometer road linking the gold fields of Diamantina and Ouro Preto to the coast. The gold once transported to Paraty was then moved by ship to Rio and from there exported to Lisbon. Later an overland route direct from Minas to Rio was established and Paraty declined, that is, until tourism in the 20th century. Situated in a huge bay with many islands and streams pouring into it, Paraty became THE coastal retreat for "Cariocas" as well as "Paulistas." It is a charming town with colonial architecture, wonderful beaches and fishing and fine restaurants (LEX guests and staff can vouch for the latter). Incidentally it became known for the best "cachaça" or sugar cane rum in those parts.

A personal aside: upper class friends in Rio encouraged me as a young scholar on a student budget doing research to join them on weekends in Paraty saying: "It's really a good deal, about $1000 USD for the weekend." That is why my first visit is with LEX. Some highlights and photos follow.

Paraty. Up at 6:30. It was a day of very heavy rain, the most so far on the trip.

Breakfast, ride into town in a zooming zodiac with Jen Martin driving into the beautiful scene of the bay and town and ship. The long quay, the main plaza with the old men playing "cirandinha" music. The small fish market, the cobblestone streets, the beautiful tiled buildings with "azulejos". Churches, tour with Chris the local guide; great lunch with Jacob, Tyrone, David and a Brazilian guest on the ship (best shore food on the trip, all kinds of shrimp, etc. icy cold beer). After lunch there was heavy rain and I did a long walk alone to the port; then the unexpected happened. Bud my boss and our Expedition Leader came zooming into the dock in a zodiac with one arm in the air with a pair of crutches and another with an envelope with cash I surmise. "Mark, got to get these to the hospital." So, I walked as fast as my legs would carry me through pouring rain to the port, crossing the river and bridge to the hospital. A guest had broken his leg on the slick "Gold Trail" (when you see the picture and imagine heavy rain and slick rocks, no surprise) but was smiling and in good spirits. I talked a bit, delivered the crutches and envelope and walked back to the port. The ride "home" to Explore was on the zodiac with Doug Gualtieri who zoomed back to the ship while seeing dolphins on the way. Check in, shower, rest. The Paraty photos follow

Our Zodiac Ride Courtesy of Jen Martin

The Beautiful Entrance into Paraty, State of Rio

Retirees do Local Folk Music – the "Cirandinha"

A Sample of 18th Century Architecture in Paraty

Staff and Ship Crew Sample Best Meal on Shore, Paraty

Icy Cold Beer Helps Wash All the Shrimp Down

The Gold Trail on a Sunny Day

FOLLOWING PARATY – ZODIACS TO ANCHIETA

ANCHIETA

Following the all too quick visit to Paraty in the morning and the wonderful lunch, Explorer moved just a few miles and then there was a very fast zodiac ride (all the drivers seem extremely confident and race right along; you must be "cool" and try not to hang on to the ropes on the side. I noticed the Lindblad veteran travelers never hung on!). The Explorer is anchored out in the bay. Anchieta is an island in the Atlantic Rain Forest, known for the its huge prison, the mutiny and prison break in 1952 and ensuing deaths. The island prison held prisoners since the 1920s, but gradually more political prisoners were added. I cannot think of a U.S. equivalent but an escape from Alcatraz might be a starter!

"Sons of the Island"

Our group was met by volunteers, "Sons of the Island," "Filhos da Ilha." This is their story: 453 prisoners revolt after planning for one year. They kill the guards, make a barrel of "cachaça" and get drunk. One hundred ride off in a boat with only a capacity of only 50; they throw the wounded over board with sharks in the waters. (At the tiny prison museum, I saw a photo of 8 or 9 sharks strung up, "one night's fishing").

The old volunteers and the official "historian" of the island latched on to me for two hours so I did not get to do the hike or the birding hike (they saw a herd of capybaras) due to the "obligation" of being ship Brazilian "cultural expert" and unofficial but busy translator. In fact, I did a lot of translating for the guests. That local "historian" who wrote the book of the prison revolt asked me to translate for him instead of his designated translator (whose English was suspect).

An Aside: on the entire trip I did a lot of translating, part of my "job," along with my area of culture and history for the various sites, and as a result saw very little nature, and that almost by accident, barring the TAIM trip at the bottom of Brazil.

So, this prison and tale are a big deal for some Brazilians, but 98 per cent of the tourists come to Anchieta from Paraty and Ubatuba for nature and the beaches. This is still part of the remaining Atlantic Rain Forest. Ironically enough I saw lots more flowers and orchids in Rio city! But there was a break in the action after the long prison tour. Later in that p.m. Tyrone Turner and I sat on chairs on the beach and we had more time to talk: there was a cool breeze in the shade of some pretty trees, a few birds by accident, and fish in the shallows. A pretty beach, but most pretty was the view from the beach past the dock to the bay and the NG Explorer.

Time with Tyrone Turner

He is a free-lance photographer and has done two or three picture stories for the magazine "National Geographic" (the text was by the same author who wrote "1491" and "1493). Cotton and Sisse are the same; National Geo today does not have as many photographers on staff, now with less money available. Most all are free - lance. Tyrone's wife is a photographer as well as teacher – she is at the Corcoran Gallery in D.C., works in the gallery and school. After this trip, he goes to Japan for Sony. As mentioned previously, Wade Davis does "around the world" jet trips. He lectures 10 hours per day and it is grueling (according to Jen).

The Explorer, Zodiacs and Arrival to Beautiful Anchieta Beach

Remains of the Famous Prison

Retiree - Volunteers, "Sons of the Island"

A Local Resident, a "Maria Farinha" Sand crab on Anchieta Beach

BACK ON BOARD - LUISA MAITE'S SÃO PAULO MUSIC

After dinner we all attended the Luisa Maité show, a "cool" new singing starlet from São Paulo, Jacob Edgar's latest discovery (and Ralph Hammellbacker the LEX music buff is on board). I would hear her again in 2014. The video of her music with São Paulo city scenes was interesting.

Luisa Maité's São Paulo Music

NEXT DAY, AT SEA, MORE PRESENTATIONS

DAVID WRIGHT – "BLACK BEARS"

At some point in the p.m. we were treated to David Wright's "Black Bears." This was not to be missed; he has won two Emmys for Planet Earth. It was filmed in northern Minnesota in the forest, the main guy dangerously trusting the bears. David is from the UK and as mentioned previously is a vegetarian; it was interesting to see him "graze" on vegan food on the trip. I would see him and Cotton, one of the other major National Geo Photographer veterans, both vegans, eating beans and such for breakfast. He was super to me and later gave me all the music Jacob had given him, a treasure trove!

BLACK BEARS, EALY, MINNESOTA. David spent one and one-half years doing the film. He is with a biologist who had tracked these bears for 15 years, gives them treats and nuts and they are very gentle with him; his head right up to theirs! Is this trust or not? Bear behavior: they slap branches and ground with the paw – a "show" or warning, but do not attack. (Maybe). Hunters in Minnesota have a deal or agreement to not take all the bears. The film showed hunters in high blinds with shotguns.

RECAP: Rich Cahill and use of hammocks in the jungle; Dennis Cornejo and plants.

I met more guests: the man was for years an executive for an international drug mfg. company, six years in Turkey and three years in Japan. He and his wife travel constantly and are booked on the newest Lindblad NG ship for its maiden voyage (Is this this Orion?). Many of these people go from one trip to another. I liked these folks, ate with them several times and both were extremely gracious to me.

Looks like I will get a chance at nature on the last day in Brazil. We ALL go to the same reserve, TAIM at Rio Grande.

Our second guest speaker (after Wade Davis) the Colombian Ex-President comes on board tomorrow at Paranaguá, the port for Curitiba. It is one hour by bus from Paranaguá to Curitiba to get the old train. (Lots of colds and sniffling around, some folks quite sick by now). It's a doozy. I'll only get it last day of trip.

Dinner that evening was interesting. One of the guests has a vial of gastritis potion bought at that colorful market in Belém do Pará in Brazil, and said it works. Note: there was conversation about Brazilian music and many guests agree with me – the 1960s were the Golden Age of Brazil music, the time of Bossa Nova and "Black Orpheus."

OCTOBER 19TH. THE MAJOR PORT OF PARANAGUÁ, BUS TO CURITIBA, TRAIN TO MORRETES, BACK TO PORT

I slept soundly for 4 hours, then dozed until 4:45 and up. Quick breakfast, shave and sandwich. To Bus 2 with David Cothrane (Bus captain).

Paranaguá is the major deep-water port in Southern Brazil, the main port for products from Curitiba and points west. Grains of all types, especially soybeans, and then automobiles. We saw lines of dump trucks with the soy and acres of parked new vehicles ready to be shipped. The docks are huge, second in size of all Brazil. It indeed was a vast truck terminal for soy etc. from far west and northern Paraná State (Iguaçu, etc.) We saw long lines of trucks stretching outside the port waiting for entrance and a chance to unload.

Heavy rain yesterday, all is very green and wet. Our comfortable bus will take us on a gradual rise to about 3000 feet through "Serra do Mar" and what remains of the Atlantic Rain Forest and in particular in this region, the Araraquara Forest ("Pinheiros do Paraná"). Lots of fog and clouds but no rain. Cool in a.m.

We saw the "Bus tubes" in Curitiba, known for its innovative public transportation system, high-rise buildings, parks, an extremely busy bus and train terminal.

The Curitiba – Morretes Train

The train to Morretes was a four-hour ride from Curitiba for 70 kilometers to the beautiful town of Morretes at sea level. However, the train was very disappointing to me – diesel, straight back uncomfortable seats and with "little character," (We are spoiled in Durango, Colorado with the steam trains running through the San Juan Mountains to the old mining town of Silverton, the charm of the Durango and Silverton Railroad.) This train was old and weathered and not comfortable. The train moved slowly through dense vegetation but was still too fast for pictures. There were not many flowers, but a few good views (for milli-seconds) of streams and one lightning quick view down to the coast and the ocean, but we definitely saw what is left of the Rain Forest. This is one of the days I would have preferred to be with the birders.

This shot from the train is of the "Pinheiro do Paraná," or the Paraná Pine tree, known in the south as the "Araraquara." The disappearance of the Atlantic Rain Forest or "A Serra do Mar" has also taken its toll on such species.

Videographer Rodrigo surprised me and wanted video with history of the train; I begged off honestly saying I did not have any knowledge other than the snippets from the train guide. The ole' pro David Barnes did it with same info and that British calm.

The ride, a blur of vegetation, was worth it at the end with a delightful visit to Morretes.

On the edge of that same Atlantic Rain Forest, it was founded in 1721, earlier inhabited by Guaraní Indians and with a minor gold rush in the area in the late 1600s. We arrived in the crowded town, charming with pretty river running through it. The name is worth the trip: the Nhambuquara River (most of the place names in this part of Southern Brazil are of the Guaraní Indian culture).

Dinner in Morretes was second best on shore for the trip (Curran's opinion); a special Paraná beef stew was delicious ["barreado"] and there were mounds of diverse types of shrimp. Icy beer. Good veggies, desserts and Brazilian coffee. The group had local folk dancing on a wooden stage in Morretes, just kind of clunky, but an interesting "retirees" choir singing in the old central city park. It was the flavor of rural southern Brazil. And there are still remnants of the 18th century colonial architecture. All in all, a very pleasant stop before the return by bus to the Port.

Curran at the Restaurant in Morretes

The "Nhambuquara" River at Morretes

There were more interesting guests at dinner that evening after Morretes: the gentleman has been with Bechtel all over the world, was a good friend of Charles Schultz, secretary of state under Reagan. He told a story when Reagan called Schultz in the middle of the night and on the spot for something in England. Just an aside: his brother did the first marrow transplant operation.

Another such personage was the gentleman who headed Merck's sales to veterinarians in the U.S. and was also on the crew team for two Olympics. He had a knee brace but danced up a storm with the "mulattas" in Rio!

I would meet and talk briefly to Ex - President Gaviria, one of our special speakers for the trip with that nice "clean" ["un español muy limpio"] Spanish of Colombia.

All this at sea following Morretes.

OCTOBER 20TH. AT SEA

FIRST PRESENTATION, CÉSAR GAVIRIA, EX-PRESIDENT OF COLOMBIA

First talk, 9:15. President César Gaviria (from Pereira in Colombia) gave a complex talk about all Latin America – economics overall and by each country. He really knows his business. Big on "democracy," "open economy" and free trade. Heavy Spanish accent in English. He liked NAFTA, praises Chile, Colombia, Mexico and Brazil for economies, but says the latter is still not truly an "open" economy. Other points of the talk:

Brazil's positives: land, sun, rain, water, with good commodity prices but lousy on corruption. Good on energy – alcohol, ethanol, oil.
Venezuela; a corrupt state and economy.
Cuba a communist country, no possibilities.
Colombia: a constitution with rights for all and it works.
He said privately he can't live in Colombia now, too dangerous for him. He had been to the Ucuengá ranch and country inn where my wife Keah and I stayed in the 1970s.

11:00S CURRAN'S LAST PRESENTATION OF THE TRIP: SWAN SONG TO BRAZIL

This is my last talk, the "swan song" for the trip. I reviewed previous talks ever so briefly, explained my research topic of Brazil's folk-popular, narrative poetry (it tells stories) "cordel" and showed images of the covers. There were many positive comments, and several wanted my small English-Portuguese Anthology. Ralph praised the talk, the right man at the right place! (Incidentally the guests liked the handouts; no one else used them on the trip, but the guests said they would read and use for reference at home. This was a carryover from professorial days in classes – the obligatory summary of the lecture.)

SUMMARY OF NOTES ON "A PORTRAIT OF BRAZIL – THE 'LITERATURA DE CORDEL'"

1. Folk-Popular Poetry (narrative) in chapbooks or pamphlets. They tell a story.
2. Came from Portugal in the 18th century, also France, Spain, Italy.
3. In Prose to the Northeast; converted to poetry by the folk-popular poets Entertainment/ teaching/ news.
4. 100,000 titles by end of the 20th century; some have sold one million copies.
5. Sold in markets, fairs, sung by poets, influenced major Brazilian writers, movies, "telenovelas."

6. Show my book: A Bilingual Anthology of Brazil's Folk – Popular Poetry: English-Portuguese."

7. The big story of "cordel" is in a new book: "Portrait of Brazil in the 20th Century: The Universe of the 'Literatura de Cordel'." (The book goes "live" at Trafford and Amazon during this trip.)

8. Orange cards to see a good example of the Brazilian woodcut which decorates the covers; Google the site.

So, the book tells of "Cordel" - a Brazilian Folk-Popular Epic in Ten Chapters or "Cantos"

1. In this we believe
2. The manifestations
3. What not to do: the wages of sin
4. Our heroes
5. Life is a struggle; life is a saga
6. We have our distractions
7. In politics we trust but do not believe
8. There is a big world out there
9. Life is getting difficult
10. This is not the end.

Up to the library for a look out; then to the bridge, my first chance since the whales).

RECAP BY TYRONE, DOUG AND BUD

Bud is with us to provide the daily plan for coming days. I sat by Javier and President César Gaviria, but the conversation was short. I gave him my book on Colombia and received a formal, quick "Thank you."

There is a nice, young reporter for "Canada News" on board; the idea is for her to write of the trip and perhaps garner future guests from Canada; she interviewed me a bit, but I was a minor character in the big story.

THE PLAN AND LATE NEWS

I'm tired. Notes. To bed. Tomorrow is our last day in Brazil. We arrive at Brazil's southernmost but major port of Rio Grande. We shall all go to TAIM Nature Reserve. Bus duty! Then a new task: Jacob Edgar had to leave the ship for duties in Madrid; I am to introduce the last musical group, the Rio Grande do Sul Jazz Quartet - "Quartcheko." It will be a late night.

OCTOBER 21. RIO GRANDE DO SUL, PORT AND BUS TO TAIM RESERVE

Up 6 a.m., slept semi-well, am a bit rested. Felt a bit refreshed. Preparation and ready to leave: mud room, by the zodiac storage, 300 level to docks. No buses; waited one-hour, Richard White set up for birds with camera and tri pod. This once again is a huge port at Rio Grande, many cargo ships, Petrobras drilling rig under repair.

Ornithologist Richard White Preparing for the TAIM Reserve.

We leave 11:15 through the huge port. Last night I rolled at sea in bed. Ships and trucks seem to be loading fertilizer. Brazil's immensity and export economy are in view. And also its deep water oil drilling.

The Huge Petrobras Oil Rig at the Port of Rio Grande do Sul

It is a one and one-half hour ride on the bus to TAIM wildlife preserve. We traveled through totally flat land, lots of agricultural crops, eucalyptus groves, rice, cattle and lands soaked from rains, the "pampa" of Brazil. All kinds of birds are in the fields: egret, caracara (Mexican eagle). Pete Poulson was on the bus, the seat behind me, an "encyclopedia" of wildlife.

RIO GRANDE AND THE "TAIM" RESERVE"

The entire group went to TAIM, like a US. Wildlife Refuge administered today by the Chico Mendes Institute. An Aside on Chico Mendes:

Chico Mendes (1944-1988) was a local union, labor leader in the Amazon Region in the 1980s. He originally was a rubber tapper in Xapuri (Acre State). My research on "cordel" deals in part with the "rubber boom" in the Amazon in the early 20th century (raw rubber before the synthetic miracle). The Indians in the Amazon had already been decimated by forced labor and disease, so Brazil's solution were the poor migrants from Brazil's Northeast, the land of "cordel." The poets chronicled unbelievably bad living conditions the twenty years prior to Chico Mendes's time. It is a long, complex and even convoluted story; in short, Chico Mendes helped organize the rubber workers and the fight for better working conditions. His role evolved to regional leader, backed by the workers' party and he became involved with the bigger question of saving the rain forest. In 1988 while fighting against a greedy rancher's efforts to log the forest and get rid of anybody in his way, Chico was on the list and was murdered by the rancher's son. Today he is considered the national symbol of Environmentalism in Brazil. Interestingly enough, this author heard more than once extreme opposition to him by Brazilians; one said he should get a "real job." It got to the point I quit bringing up the topic.

TAIM is located on a narrow strip of land between the Atlantic and Mirim Lake, renowned for 30 different mammals and 250 species of birds (on one LEX trip the naturalists were ecstatic seeing more than 100 species alone in one day!) LEX brought lunch and I liked it, big chicken sandwiches and salad.

We did three "zones" by bus, some walking. (David Barnes is bus captain.) I served a bit as translator. (There were innumerable times as translator on the ship; the guests knew I did this in Fernando de Noronha, Salvador, Rio, Anchieta, Paraty, the train from Curitiba to Morretes, and Paranaguá and Quartcheko. And for Dr. Cary's blood work on board.)

It was a wonderful day with wonderful sights:

1. Forest, enormous Fica tree ("figueira"), orchids, ants. I saw the first capybara nursing a babe along the way.
2. Highway and ponds: Brazilian alligator ["jacaré" - an aside on the beaches in Rio: when you are body surfing you are "fazendo jacaré" or making like an alligator], and many capybaras. I saw what I thought was a brilliant red "new find" - it turned out to be a Vermillion Flycatcher! (Must have traveled from Southern Arizona! Ha!)
3. Wade through water, like walking Bear River Refuge in Utah; water birds, stream bed full of birds.

I am generous with the photos – an amazing excursion!

First Sighting – Female Capybara Nursing Baby

The Enormous "Fica" Tree, TAIM Reserve

One of the Many Tropical Birds in the Refuge.

The "Jacaré" or Brazilian Alligator

We waded across several fields to get last chance views of the birds; this photo also has a "rare bird" – cultural staffer Curran looking like a naturalist. Dream on!

HOME TO EXPLORER AND THE RIO GRANDE DO SUL JAZZ QUARTET

The bus trip home of one and one-half hours seemed long. There was a quick shower and I'm back on duty: meeting and introducing the Rio Grande do Sul (Porto Alegre) Jazz Quartet. I was first introduced to Quartcheko – Júlio Rizzo, band leader and trombone, Luciano accordion, Hilton guitar, and Ricardo drums. I ate dinner with them and their agent and translated. Then music on the back deck. I translate titles of selections in English to the guests as they are performed. Personally, the musicians were all great, but I loved that Rio Grande do Sul great accordion!

The Brazilian Jazz Band on Board the Explorer – "Quartchecko"

OCTOBER 22, AT SEA TOWARD URUGUAY

At sea. Late that night there was a staff party in the crew cabin next door, all were there. I felt like a bit of an interloper. Lots of stories, jokes; they all know each other. I left at 11:00; it went on for a while, great camaraderie by all.

WORST TIME. I am on the internet most of the day dealing with Argentina Reciprocity paperwork. At this point it may be okay, but I was exhausted dealing with it from the a.m. to 4:00 p.m. Talked to Ralph and he said Lindblad would handle any problems. There will be much more about this later: the essence of the problem was that when I did the Argentina Reciprocity document (like a visa) on the internet from home in Colorado I printed it all EXCEPT the last page with the bar code. Without the bar code page, no deal! It is very difficult to explain the terrible stress on me of the moment, and it will all be another of those "rookie" travel mistakes.

A distraction was the final talk by the Colombia president: his take on drugs in Latin America - build schools not prisons, and he should know. It was a small distraction from my unsolved problem. He says of growing of coca, etc. in Latin America: not prohibition of drugs, but regulation.

There would be more distraction the following day with an amazing new adventure for me: Uruguay - Montevideo and a "gaucho" ranch or "estancia."

Announcements on Board before Uruguay

We received notice to settle our Visa and Internet bill.

The plan for the last day in Buenos Aires: move guest luggage, go on the day tour of Buenos Aires, lunch, tango show and to airport. There will be no time to shower. Take back pack and be ready for the airport.

OCTOBER 23 – THE BEGINNING OF ANOTHER WORLD BEYOND BRAZIL

Before continuing with Montevideo, the capital of Uruguay, and the "gaucho" ranch, there are some thoughts and emotions important to express. Of course, the main purpose of my "gig" on the Explorer in 2013, a wonderful retirement adventure, was to share expertise, enthusiasm and knowledge of Brazil. Uruguay and Argentina, both new to me, were really a "bonus" and represented a new life experience.

I had studied about Uruguay in graduate school for the Ph.D. and remembered its fame as a truly democratic country in Latin America priding itself on that aspect of its history. We read two or three works of its literature, but honestly, they made little impression on me. My main recollection was that it possessed a high ethnicity of European stock and was a much smaller version of Argentina. And Montevideo the same, a smaller version of Buenos Aires. And of course, that the country pulled the surprise upset of Brazil in the inaugural World Cup in the Maracanã Stadium in Rio in 1950.

The fact we would be taken to a real-life working Uruguayan ranch or "estancia" was a huge bonus for me – the ranch country and "gauchos" we had studied at Saint Louis University were those of Argentina. On a later trip I might have impressed one of the Argentine naturalists on the Explorer by mentioning I indeed had read the entire novel "El Gaucho Martín Fierro;" evidently only voracious readers, courageous or slightly esoteric Argentines, had done the same in recent times. I suspect it was required reading in the high schools and bet there was an Argentine version of "Cliff Notes" for the less inspired students. The spirit of the novel remains iconic in Argentina – the free "cowboy" of the Pampas. However, it is extremely important on a personal basis, perhaps even life-changing.

As a teenager in Abilene High School (Kansas) in the late 1950s I received my introduction to foreign languages (after two years of Latin) in the Spanish classes by a truly traditional "schoolmarm" dedicating her life to her students. We had a Spanish Club and an annual Spanish banquet, and on that occasion during senior year I played "Malagueña" on a Kay electric guitar (sacrilege!) but remembered our guest speakers.

Two young fellows dressed in leather boots with spurs, the bellowing Argentine trousers ("bombachas"), leather belts and long knives attached, entertained us with their stories of time spent in Argentina as small-town 4-H exchange students (you lived on a farm or ranch and did some work). Right away I decided that I wanted to learn more Spanish (I was already a 4-H'er) and go to Argentina and live that experience. There was a detour – study in Mexico City, travel in Guatemala, the Ph.D. at St. Louis, a life-time teaching career focusing on Spain and Brazil – and only 50 years later did I meet up with any real "gauchos." All the above is to express my barely contained enthusiasm for the "estancia" and Uruguay.

SPANISH LANGUAGE AND THE EXCURSION TO MONTEVIDEO

An added note: I know a fair amount of Spanish, after all, the Ph.D. was not all theory in libraries, but this would be a baptism in the version of Castilian spoke in the south of South America, that of Uruguay, Argentina (and incidentally, Chile). Instead of "calle," they say "cajje." My version of the spoken language, really a bit eclectic, is based on New World Spanish, but primarily spoken in Mexico, Guatemala and Colombia (the Colombians claim to have the "purest" and "best" Spanish in the Hemisphere including the Caro y Cuervo Linguistic Institute to back it up, but evidently have not consulted the Argentinians).

The main plaza of Montevideo is dedicated to General José Artigas. The general fought for years for an independent Uruguay, first against Argentina and Buenos Aires, then the Spanish Monarchy which had moved the viceroyalty to Montevideo after Argentina became independent, then the Portuguese attacking the eastern provinces. He ended his life banished to Paraguay, but it was his life-long struggle for Uruguay that earned him fame.

General José Artigas, Main Plaza, Montevideo

In the main plaza of Uruguay behind staffer Curran is one of Montevideo's most famous buildings – Palacio Salvo, built on the site of the old "confitaria" where the famous tango "La Cumparsita" was composed. Its architecture is called "eclectic" (a similar building was first constructed in Buenos Aires, a model for this one) and it is noted for its height, and the top was originally intended to be a light house, then with antennae now taken down.

Below the statue is the mausoleum of Artigas with a national guard and changing of the guard ceremony. The uniforms hark back to the 19th century and the battles for Independence. On several occasions in Montevideo we saw grade school groups on city outings and noticed the school uniform with the white "smock" as well as the ethnicity of the children. For sure we were no longer in Brazil!

Another major sight was in Prado Park with this famous sculpture called "la Carreta." The wagon and oxen cart symbolize the frontier spirit and "drive" into the interior of Uruguay and its own "pampa" or plains ranching country. There is a real parallel to our own conestoga covered wagons on the way West in the 19th century. And we will see a similar pheomenon to the "carreta" in Argentina as well.

The rather modest blue building, the national soccer stadium must be noted: Uruguay made soccer history with that world cup victory in Rio's huge Maracanã Stadium (200,000 capacity with standing room), built to be a monument to Brazilian "futebol" and deflated in 1950 by tiny Uruguay.

And lastly but not least important we saw the National Legislature Building in Montevideo, a truly amazing and beautiful architectural monument to Uruguay's history of democracy. It is neo-classical in style and was inaugurated in 1925, 100 years after Uruguay's Independence. The building in style, size and grandeur rivals anything in Washington, D.C.

"LA ESTANCIA" – "LA RÁBIDA"

Exiting Montevideo to the Uruguayan plains or "pampa," we had a long drive into the ranch by eucalyptus groves with large herds of cattle and incidentally a Harrier hawk.

"Gauchos" on horseback with flags of Uruguay greeted us, riding fast along the bus. An introduction of refreshment of beer and wine was followed by a long talk by the widow of the owner of 10 years with a Basque name. The time before a huge "asado" or barbecue lunch was dedicated to a long hayrack ride to the edge of the Río de la Plata and its beach. The Río de la Plata with its brown water seemed like an ocean; the sand beach very wide.

We all enjoyed a great churrasco dinner, "salchicha," "sweet breads," salad bar and then grilled pork, lamb, chicken and "colita de cuadril,' the best beef cut they said. Beer and wine were served. All was followed by incredibly fresh and tasty strawberries and cream.

During lunch there was a great Gaucho music show (with canned music but okay) but fine dancing, macho "gaucho" cowboy and girl, and "boleadores," the Gaucho "lasso" choreographed into a drum show. After lunch the ole' Kansas farm boy got to milk a cow, very successfully I might add. There were horseback rides and a quaint "thrill" - they dragged people on a big leather sheet behind horses. A long ride, most guests dozing, ensued to Montevideo and back "home" to Explorer. "Estancia" photos follow.

LEX Group Greeting the "Gauchos"

Curran the 4-Her's Dream of Being a Gaucho

The Ranch "Asado" or Barbecue for LEX

174

The Famous River Plate – Río de la Plata – Coast of Uruguay

Uruguayan Dance Show with "Gaucho" and Young Lady

Farm Boy Milks Cow After 55 Years

BACK ON BOARD, MORE STRESS

This is on me; I don't know how others would have handled it. After that wonderful distraction on the ranch in Uruguay there was a return to the stress coming up. All this was regarding the damned Argentine Reciprocity form alluded to days earlier, in effect a visa paper with the bar code. I had printed it all out at home, I thought, but did not get to the last page with the bar code.

I spent two hours on the staff computer trying to find the Argentine page, get on and print the document. I was full of absolute fear and tense. I had been informed by ship staff that if I did not find the document, LEX and the ship would be fined by the Argentine government, and I would have to pay several hundred dollars, and in cash, and if I did not have the money, would have to borrow it from friends. This information was passed on to me in the form of an ULTIMATUM!

In desperation I sent an e-mail to my wife Keah, still in Colorado, and fortunately she was home and answered. She looked up forms I left at home, found the original password for the Argentine Reciprocity form, I gave it to Patrik the ship Hotel Manager, he went right on the computer, printed the form and all was well.

I sent another email to Keah: "The user name and password from you via email saved the day!" When I got home to Mesa I made about a dozen copies of it. It was a veritable NIGHTMARE. Don't think I have had such tension and stress in my young life.

RELIEF, RELIEF, RELIEF

After completing the paper with Patrik the Hotel Manager, I walked into the dining room, sat with a favorite guest couple and drank two or three glasses of wine. To cabin, pack, notes, to bed.

OCTOBER 24TH. BUENOS AIRES, THE LAST STOP

Slept soundly 10 – 2, dozed after that. Sore throat coming on. Up about 6, shave, shower, final pack. Coffee, pastry and fruit.

7:00. All staff bring luggage down, quite a maneuver, bags to destination by color code on stickers. Got up a real sweat! Then breakfast with Richard White, my ornithologist "roommate."

To room, gather up all my stuff. Pick up passport from purser (whew!), off and goodbyes to some passengers and to some staff.

Lucho, David Barnes, Doug Gualtieri and Bud stay on; some go home for R and R, others to other ships. It truly is like a LEX- NATIONAL GEO navy.

Bye to Bud Lenhausen my first EL; I said, "Some glitches," and he said, "It's your first time." (I asked David Barnes if he got it all right the first time; he said "no.")

But Ralph H., ever friendly, said he wanted to hear from me in six days. I'm sure he wants me back in 2014. More later on this.

Aside: a memory from the ship: never in my life did I enjoy so many lattes, cappuccinos, and espressos. Wired!

To the Buenos Aires port, through the port (huge) to buses to terminal outside. Bus 3 for city tour and lunch at "Almacén" for Tango show.

Now at 6:30 a.m., boarding buses at 7:30; I am sick with that nasty cold and exhausted.

BUENOS AIRES

Where to begin? This is a major world city in many ways: the metropolitan area (it is an autonomous region of Argentina) is 17 million, second largest city in Latin America after Mexico City. São Paulo is a close third! But BA (I hate that abbreviation!) is oh so different from either of them. Buenos Aires is highly cosmopolitan, the most "European" of all cities in Latin America, primarily of Spanish and Italian peoples, but many others from all over Europe including Latin America's largest Jewish population of around 250,000!

It is without doubt the major cultural city of Latin America with more theaters than even New York! Many orchestras are world class including the Symphonic Orchestra of Buenos Aires; the Teatro Colón is a bastion of theater and opera. Some (other Latin Americans) say the "porteños" are arrogant, thinking of themselves as superior to other Latin Americans; I join that opinion, but held perhaps with good reason.

The important thing for me is the total contrast to Brazil and in particular Rio de Janeiro – night and day! The main avenue 9th of Julio, the nattily dressed men (dark business suits) and women (latest styles from Europe), the business atmosphere of the city and especially the spoken Spanish make for a place that knows where it's going. Tropical Rio with beaches, carnival and "futebol" (Argentina has the latter and has of late "whomped" the Brazilian teams, Explorer staff reminded me of this, mentioning Leonardo Messi among others!).

The city of Carlos Gardel the tango singer and the tango clubs and the colorful neighborhood of San Telmo would be on our excursions, but a more familiar Argentinian reality, one I indeed had studied in graduate school, came first. The Recoleta Cemetery with Eva Peron's grave and the Casa Rosada of Juan Perón and Evita's fame would come later as would the contemporary story of the Italian-Argentinian Archbishop who would become Pope Francis.

LA RECOLETA CEMETERY

A main stop on all the tourist maps is the Recoleta Cemetery where Evita Perón is buried. It is safe to say she is the most famous woman (until perhaps Mexico's Frida Kahlo or even Salma Hayek of recent days) in all Latin America. This is not a university classroom or lecture hall – the short version is that Evita, a radio singer in the 1940s, met Juan Perón the rising star of the Argentine military who would become president and dictator of Argentina espousing the urban, industrial revolution and labor class ("los descamisados") over the old, failing rural "estancia" upper class, become his mistress, then his wife, and finally his political partner (the female branch of the Peronista party and its social – welfare sector) and finally "Saint Evita" tragically succumbing to cancer in 1952. "Peronismo" is still a major force in Argentinian politics (one pundit called it "political necrophilia") and Evita is still "Santa Evita."

Evita Peron's Message to "Disciples" from Her Tomb

"WITH IT" BUENOS AIRES

As the LEX excursion wove its way through Buenos Aires I was on the lookout for something else: that avant-garde, on the cutting edge, "porteño" vision of the good life. And I accidentally found it, first outside Recoleta Cemetery where a TV camera crew just finished doing a commercial with a beautiful, blond "porteño" model (she perhaps with a Gucci handbag and her smart phone):

TV Commercial and Model in Buenos Aires

Then there suddenly appeared a simple billboard advertising BIC plastic razors which goes a long way to explain Argentinian – "Porteño" Spanish plus the "get with it and be with it" local attitude: the local "tú" or second person familiar pronoun with the regional variant pronunciation: "tenés" or "usás" translated: "Get with it!" or "Get an attitude!" and "Use the New BIC Flex 4."

A curiosity perhaps but another way to show that Buenos Aires does not lag Central Park in New York was this professional "dog-walker" in the Recoleta section of town. Our bus tour guide, when I raised the issue and called folks' attention to him, was "You can make a good living in Buenos Aires doing this, maybe $1000 USD per month." It was not clear if he had the mandatory "pooper scooper" or "doggy bags" of U.S. parks, but one can only assume. I'm sure there was a "system."

After Recoleta Cemetery and residential district and Palermo the high-end swank region of Buenos Aires, we got into the traffic on its huge and largest avenue, the "9 de Julio" Avenue, billed as "the widest avenue in the world." Of note is the image of Eva Perón on the "news" flow of the distant skyscraper; on another day it was the advertisement for the Ricky Martin show soon to come. I apologize for not showing all fourteen lanes of traffic plus the bus lanes, but you get the idea.

LA PLAZA DE MAYO AND LA CASA ROSADA

Next was the national palace in Buenos Aires' main historic plaza, the Plaza de Mayo, sometime official place for presidential happenings, most famous for the appearance of Eva from the upper balcony and in movie fame "Don't Cry for me Argentina!" I studied and read of the Perón times, of Juan and Evita, of her death, of his being ousted by the military, his comeback after being sheltered by Franco in Spain and his second wife of less renown, Isabel; there are hundreds of books on the subject. This was the scene.

La Casa Rosada, Plaza de Mayo, Buenos Aires

In the same plaza is the homage - statue of General San Martín of Argentine Independence from Spain, he of the fame of crossing the Andes with mules, horses and soldiers and surprising the Spaniards in Chile, winning that battle, and his famous encounter with that other guy, General Simón Bolívar. Bolívar was of course the leader in independence coming from the North, from Venezuela and after major battles in Colombia (told in one of my books) meeting San Martín in Lima for a truly historic encounter. Historians since have speculated, but the fact is San Martín acquiesced to Bolívar, returned to Argentina and retirement in France, leaving Simón Bolívar as South America's renowned Liberator. Sad. But not totally sad, his remains are in the national cathedral of Buenos Aires. An honor guard marches in on occasion with a salute to the fallen hero.

Statue of General San Martín, Liberator of Argentina from Spain

THE NATIONAL CATHEDRAL

The Neo-Classic Façade of the National Cathedral. One might recall that the Viceroyalty of La Plata came late to Spanish American History in the 18th century, and its main edifices would not be that Baroque exuberance of Mexico City or Lima, but the more "refined" Neo-Classic of Bogotá and Buenos Aires. If one can succeed in safe fully crossing the bus traffic, the Cathedral awaits.

The Neo-Classic Cathedral of Buenos Aires

Of great import, and hopefully fact, not rumor, is that current Pope Francis when he was Archbishop of Buenos Aires, following his Jesuit (modern that is, not the old timers') beliefs, lived in a small apartment in a modest two-story building to the side of the Cathedral. We were told it was "behind the statue." And of interest on this trip to Brazil and Argentina was the first TV report of Francis's election, not from Buenos Aires, but from a reporter on Copacabana Beach in Rio – the TV "bet" was that a Brazilian Cardinal for sure would be Pope. Just another "accident" in Brazilian history!

Perhaps the Former Archbishop now Pope Francis's Residence in Buenos Aires

SAN TELMO

The next stop on the excursion would be the "kitsch" artistic district of San Telmo, a true delight and link to the old Italian district and the development of the Tango. On the way, Curran spotted yet another scene the guides studiously ignored but which is extremely important to modern Argentina. Relegated to an ignominious dirt-gravel incline under a large freeway was this scene depicted in my blurry picture (the bus traveled fast and did not stop for a closer view nor did the tour guide want to mention the place) – tiny flags with the names of the "disappeared" leftist students during the military regime and the "Dirty War" of the 1960s and 1970s. Argentine generals ruled with an iron fist emulating their colleagues in Chile (Pinochet) and Brazil. A few years prior to this visit in 2013 the most famous place in Argentine history and politics was indeed the "Plaza de Mayo" where the mothers of the deceased and disappeared students walked each Thursday afternoon wearing white scarves, each with the name of the missing son, protesting their disappearance and asking the military for justice. In 2016 all that remained were the white painted footprints of the ladies in the Plaza.

The Underpass Homage to the "Desaparecidos," Buenos Aires

The traditional Buenos Aires, "Porteño" Tango hats are for sale in shops in San Telmo.

The Equally Renowned Argentine Bikini

The "kitsch" mannequins of Diego Maradona the Soccer King, Evita Perón and Carlos Gardel of Buenos Aires tango fame highlight a roof in Caminito Street in San Telmo, and are followed by the hired tango dancers; he reminded me of Al Pacino.

Our final moment in Buenos Aires was the outstanding tango show at the "Viejo Almacén" or "Old Store" in San Telmo, the LEX guests getting to see a top of the line Tango troupe.

THE BUENOS AIRES AIRPORT AND DEPARTURE

After the show and lunch, it was off to the airport. Buenos Aires airport was sparkling new, antiseptic, with an icy cold AC, what a difference from São Paulo. The latter seemed ages ago at the beginning of my trip to Explorer (note: there was a protest outside the airport, we were lucky to get through and not be delayed, perhaps missing the international flight). I found myself asking myself "Where exactly am I?" I guess I must be somewhere between the São Paulo Airport, Belém do Pará, Salvador da Bahia, Ilhéus, Rio, Montevideo and Buenos Aires. The latter was a great cosmopolitan city, but Rio has the beaches, the ocean and Carnival. The famous Río de la Plata seemed like a "muddy inland sea."

EPILOGUE

LEX trip planner Ralph Hammellbacker said he wanted an answer from me right away for the 2014 Explorer Trip from Brazil (starting in Salvador da Bahia) to Buenos Aires. He was very positive and enthused over the work in 2013. I asked for a week, got home, rested up and sent them a "yes." Hence, Volume II to come!

So ended the first chapter of the great retirement "gig" with LEX-NATIONAL GEO. When one walks down the stairway exiting Explorer there are a multitude of emotions, that is, when you are a part-timer and a first timer. In this case Ralph had indicated a desire for me to be available in the aforementioned trip in 2014, so goodbyes and nostalgia were put on hold. Volume II will treat the trip from 2014 and a surprise opportunity in 2016. Much more emotion will accompany those goodbyes. Now however is the time to tie up "loose ends" from 2013.

There can be no doubt that literally I "started at the top;" nothing can match staff-cultural speaker on the Flagship of the Lindblad Fleet, the Explorer. As David Barnes said one night on Explorer, "You get to travel the world and I hope the young naturalists realize what a gift that is." I had a small taste of that cake. What can one compare to Belém do Pará, Fernando de Noronha, Salvador da Bahia, Ilhéus, Rio de Janeiro, Paraty, Anchieta, Rio Grande in Brazil, Montevideo and the "Estancia" in Uruguay and the great Buenos Aires? Sharing my love, enthusiasm and knowledge of Brazil plus translating in both Portuguese and Spanish "earned my keep" on the trip. The people you meet – the Expedition Leaders, the Naturalists, the Distinguished Guest Speakers, and not to mention the amazing people that travel on these ships - all this is unforgettable. But the experience of learning the ropes (somewhat) and life as a staff member on Explorer and its shore excursions is indeed a lifelong memory. I shall try to add to the experience, the joy, excitement and sometimes difficult moments of two more golden opportunities on that ship in Volume II of this narrative.

ABOUT THE AUTHOR

Mark Curran is a retired professor from Arizona State University where he worked from 1968 to 2011. He taught Spanish and Portuguese and their respective cultures. His research specialty was Brazil and its "popular poetry in verse" or the "literatura de cordel," and he has published many articles in research reviews and now some sixteen books related to the "cordel" in Brazil, the United States and Spain. Other books done during retirement are of either an autobiographic nature – "The Farm" or "Coming of Age with the Jesuits" - or reflect classes taught at ASU in Luso-Brazilian Civilization, Latin American Civilization or Spanish taught at ASU. The latter are in the series "Stories I Told My Students:" books on Brazil, Colombia, Guatemala, Mexico, Portugal and Spain. "Letters from Brazil" is an early experiment combining reporting and fiction, and "A Professor Takes to the Sea – Learning the Ropes on the National Geographic Explorer" is a chronicle of a retirement adventure with Lindblad Expeditions - National Geographic Explorer.

Published Books

A Literatura de Cordel. Brasil. 1973

Jorge Amado e a Literatura de Cordel. Brasil. 1981

A Presença de Rodolfo Coelho Cavalcante na Moderna Literatura de Cordel. Brasil. 1987

La Literatura de Cordel – Antología Bilingüe – Español y Portugués. España. 1990

Cuíca de Santo Amaro Poeta-Repórter da Bahia. Brasil. 1991

História do Brasil em Cordel. Brasil. 1998

Cuíca de Santo Amaro – Controvérsia no Cordel. Brasil. 2000

Brazil's Folk-Popular Poetry – "a Literatura de Cordel" – a Bilingual Anthology in English and Portuguese. USA. 2010

The Farm – Growing Up in Abilene, Kansas, in the 1940s and the 1950s. USA. 2010

Retrato do Brasil em Cordel. Brasil. 2011

Coming of Age with the Jesuits. USA. 2012

Peripécias de um Pesquisador "Gringo" no Brasil nos Anos 1960 ou À Cata de Cordel." USA. 2012

Adventures of a 'Gringo' Researcher in Brazil in the 1960s or In Search of "Cordel." USA. 2012

A Trip to Colombia – Highlights of Its Spanish Colonial Heritage. USA. 2013

Travel, Research and Teaching in Guatemala and Mexico – In Quest of the Pre-Columbian Heritage

        Volume I – Guatemala. 2013

        Volume II – Mexico. USA. 2013

A Portrait of Brazil in the Twentieth Century – The Universe of the "Literatura de Cordel." USA. 2013

Fifty Years of Research on Brazil – A Photographic Journey. USA. 2013

Relembrando - A Velha Literatura de Cordel e a Voz dos Poetas. USA. 2014

Aconteceu no Brasil – Crônicas de um Pesquisador Norte Americano no Brasil II, USA. 2015

It Happened in Brazil – Chronicles of a North American Researcher in Brazil II. USA. 2015

Diário de um Pesquisador Norte-Americano no Brasil III. USA. 2016

Diary of a North American Researcher in Brazil III. USA. 2016

Letters from Brazil. A Cultural-Historical Narrative Made Fiction. USA. 2017.

A Professor Takes to the Sea – Learning the Ropes on the National Geographic Explorer

        Volume I. "Epic South America – 2013"

        USA. 2018

Professor Curran lives in Mesa, Arizona, and spends part of the year in Colorado. He is married to Keah Runshang Curran and they have one daughter Kathleen who lives in Albuquerque, New Mexico. Her documentary film "Greening the Revolution" was presented most recently in the Sonoma Film Festival in California, this after other festivals in Milan, Italy and New York City. Katie was named best female director in the Oaxaca Film Festival in Mexico.

The author's e-mail address is: profmark@asu.edu

His website address is: www.currancordelconnection.com

Printed in the United States
By Bookmasters